ESCAPE
THE COMING
NIGHT

VOLUME 4

Dr. David Jeremiah

with Dr. David Jeremiah

CONTENTS

About Dr. David Jeremiah and Turning Point 4

About This Study Guide 5

Introduction. 7

35. The Collapse of the World Market
    Revelation 18:1-24 9

36. The Marriage Supper of the Lamb
    Revelation 19:1-10 23

37. The Second Coming of Christ
    Revelation 19:11-21 35

38. The Thousand Year Reign of Christ
    Revelation 20:1-10 49

39. The Great White Throne Judgment
    Revelation 20:11-15 61

40. The New Heaven and the New Earth
    Revelation 21:1-22:5 75

41. What Will We Do in Heaven?
    Revelation 21:1-22:5 89

42. What to Do Until Then
    Revelation 22:6-16 101

43. The Last Invitation in the Bible
    Revelation 22:17-21 113

Resources 126

Price List 128

ABOUT
DR. DAVID JEREMIAH
AND TURNING POINT

D r. David Jeremiah is the founder of Turning Point, a ministry committed to providing Christians with sound Bible teaching relevant to today's changing times through radio and television broadcasts, audio series, and books. Dr. Jeremiah's common-sense teaching on topics such as family, prayer, worship, angels, and biblical prophecy forms the foundation of Turning Point.

David and his wife, Donna, reside in El Cajon, California, where he is the senior pastor of Shadow Mountain Community Church and chancellor of San Diego Christian College. David and Donna have four children and six grandchildren.

In 1982, Dr. Jeremiah brought the same solid teaching to San Diego television that he shares weekly with his congregation. Shortly thereafter, Turning Point expanded its ministry to radio. Dr. Jeremiah's inspiring messages can now be heard worldwide on radio and television.

Because Dr. Jeremiah desires to know his listening audience, he travels nationwide holding "A Night of Encouragement" ministry rallies and Spiritual Enrichment conferences that touch the hearts and lives of many people. According to Dr. Jeremiah, "At some point in time, everyone reaches a turning point; and for every person, that moment is unique, an experience to hold onto forever. There's so much changing in today's world that sometimes it's difficult to choose the right path. Turning Point offers people an understanding of God's Word as well as the opportunity to make a difference in their lives."

Dr. Jeremiah has authored numerous books, including *Escape the Coming Night* (Revelation), *The Handwriting on the Wall* (Daniel), *Overcoming Loneliness, What the Bible Says About Angels, The Power of Encouragement, Prayer—The Great Adventure, God in You* (Holy Spirit), *Gifts from God* (Parenting), *Jesus' Final Warning, When Your World Falls Apart, Slaying the Giants in Your Life, My Heart's Desire, Sanctuary, The Things That Matter, Life Wide Open, The Prayer Matrix, Searching for Heaven on Earth,* and *The Secret of the Light.*

ABOUT THIS STUDY GUIDE

The purpose of this Turning Point study guide is to reinforce Dr. David Jeremiah's dynamic, in-depth teaching on the Book of Revelation and to aid the reader in applying biblical truth to his or her daily life. This study guide is designed to be used in conjunction with Dr. Jeremiah's *Escape the Coming Night* audiocassette series, but it may be used by itself for personal or group Bible study.

STRUCTURE OF THE LESSONS

Each lesson is based on one of the tapes in the *Escape the Coming Night* audiocassette series and focuses on specific passages in the Bible. Each lesson is composed of the following elements:

• *Outline*

The outline at the beginning of the lesson gives a clear, concise picture of the passage being studied and provides a helpful framework for readers as they listen to Dr. Jeremiah's teaching.

• *Overview*

The overview summarizes Dr. Jeremiah's teaching on the passage being studied in the lesson. Readers should refer to the biblical passages in their own Bibles as they study the overview.

• *Application*

This section contains a variety of questions designed to help readers dig deeper into the lesson and the Scriptures, and to apply the lesson to their daily lives. For Bible study groups or Sunday school classes, these questions will provide a springboard for group discussion and interaction.

• *Did You Know?*

This section presents a fascinating fact, historical note, or insight that adds a point of interest to the preceding lesson.

USING THIS GUIDE FOR GROUP STUDY

The lessons in this study guide are suitable for Sunday school classes, small-group studies, elective Bible studies, or home Bible study groups. Each person in the group should have his or her own study guide.

When possible, the study guide should be used with the corresponding tape series. You may wish to assign the study guide as homework prior to the meeting of the group and then use the meeting time to listen to the tape and discuss the lesson.

FOR CONTINUING STUDY

A complete catalog of Dr. Jeremiah's materials for personal and group study is available through Turning Point. To obtain a catalog, additional study guides, or more information about Turning Point, call 1-800-947-1993 or write to: Turning Point, P.O. Box 3838, San Diego, CA 92163.

Dr. Jeremiah's *Turning Point* radio broadcast is currently heard on more than 1000 national and international radio outlets. Contact Turning Point for radio and television program times and stations in your area.

ESCAPE THE COMING NIGHT

INTRODUCTION

Everyone has been through a late-afternoon thunderstorm on a scorching summer day. While the wind picks up and the sky changes from blue to black, you haul in the lawn furniture and close the windows. Once the cat is safely inside, you sit back and wait for the proverbial bottom to fall out. And fall it does. You turn on lights in the house not only to dispel the darkness but so you'll know when the power goes out. While you kneel down with a towel to soak up the rain blowing under the front door, you whisper a confessional prayer: "Lord, I won't complain about the summer heat ever again if You'll get me through this storm."

Then, as suddenly as the summer ritual began, it's over. The rain slackens to a drizzle, the black sky begins a transition back to blue, and the air outside feels fifteen degrees cooler. The yard is strewn with leafy branches and the potted plants from your neighbor's front porch, but that appears to be the worst of it. Up go the windows and in comes the cool, sweet smell of rain-washed air. The rest of the day and evening will be a delight. "If it takes a storm to refresh the world," you think, "then I guess it's worth it."

What that picture lacks in parallel it makes up for in purpose— it is going to take a giant storm to wash the earth clean and make it a suitable eternal home for the redeemed of God. That, in essence, is what we have learned from the Book of Revelation. A storm called the Great Tribulation is brewing just over the horizon. It is going to thrash planet earth with never-seen fury in order to wash the staleness of unrighteousness and rebellion out of the air. Only after that storm has done its work will the planet experience the refreshing of which the prophets of old spoke: a time when we will go out in joy and be led forth in peace, when the mountains and hills will burst into song, when the trees of the field will clap their hands (Isaiah 55:12).

The first three volumes of our series on the Book of Revelation told the story of the storm—and what a storm it will be. At the hands of man and the devil (but with the permission of God), the earth undergoes seven years of tribulation which become a judgment upon all who have rebelled against God and His Son. When the storm subsides, God removes from earth all those who do not worship Him and throws open the windows of the world to allow justice and peace and joy to fill the air. In this final volume of the series on Revelation, we pick up John's vision at that point.

Christ and His Church are joined together and they return to earth at the end of the Tribulation. The Antichrist is destroyed, Satan is bound, and the King of Kings establishes a thousand-year reign of peace on earth. The final judgment of all unbelievers from all ages is followed by the renovation of the earth and the revealing of the New Jerusalem, the eternal dwelling place of the redeemed.

The storm the earth must go through will be severe, but it will be worth it—to arrive at a place where no storm will ever be seen again. As you study the final chapters of Revelation, make sure that you will be among those safe in heaven while the storm on earth rages. God only offers one way to escape that storm—by hiding in the Lord Jesus Christ. May you be found in Him both now and forever.

THE COLLAPSE OF THE WORLD MARKET

Revelation 18:1-24

In this lesson the destruction of the world's economic systems is described.

You will find more in-depth information on this lesson in the book *Escape the Coming Night*, chapter 15, pages 195-199.

OUTLINE

In a global economy, when one major nation catches an "economic cold," the rest of the world sneezes as well. We live in an era of global markets, and they will be tightly consolidated under the Antichrist. Therefore, when he falls, the entire world market falls with him.

I. **The Reasons for the Judgment of Babylon**
  A. Babylon Is Judged Because of Her Iniquity
  B. Babylon Is Judged Because of Her Influence
  C. Babylon Is Judged Because of Her Infidelity
  D. Babylon Is Judged Because of Her Inhumanity

II. **The Reality of the Judgment of Babylon**

III. **The Reactions to the Judgments of Babylon**
  A. The Monarchs of the Earth Will Mourn
  B. The Merchants of the Earth Will Mourn
  C. The Mariners Will Mourn

IV. **The Rejoicing Over the Judgment of Babylon**

V. **Our Response to the Judgment of Babylon**

Befvre beginning an in-depth study of Revelation 18, it will be helpful to remember that chapters 17 and 18 are parenthetical in the flow of the chronology of the book. The end of chapter 16 described the seventh bowl judgment (16:17-21), the details of which are continued in chapter 19. Chapters 17 and 18 present information which help us better understand the final events of the Great Tribulation..

Chapter 17, for example, painted a startling picture of a worldwide religious system which will arise in the end times and will be "sanctioned" by the Antichrist—before he turns on it and destroys it in the final days of the Great Tribulation. Chapter 18 continues the theme of "Babylon" (begun in chapter 17), but this time, rather than the religious ramifications, the economic and commercial aspects of this end-times world system are laid out. But even this system is not able to stand, and chapter 18 portrays its destruction just before the second coming of Christ.

Reports have surfaced in recent years that the government of Iraq wants to rebuild the ancient city of Babylon and a replica of the Tower of Babel. Their purpose would be primarily historical and cultural. But many Bible students think there would be another reason for the city to be rebuilt—perhaps unknown to the leaders of Iraq. They believe that Babylon will one day become the epicenter of the world's economic and commercial activities. The Book of Revelation doesn't tell us how or when Babylon is going to be rebuilt, but it does say in chapter 18 it is going to be destroyed. Babylon will become, prior to its destruction, the third city out of which the Antichrist will operate during the Tribulation: Rome will be the political base, Jerusalem the religious base, and Babylon the commercial and financial base.

Babylon is the most frequently mentioned city in the Bible besides Jerusalem, occurring more than 260 times. Babylon is always presented as a place which functions in opposition to God. That was the original purpose of the Tower of Babel in Genesis— to prove man's independence from the controlling influence of God. That spirit, while not called "Babylon" in our modern world, is still very much present. In Daniel 4:30 we find king Nebuchadnezzar saying, "Is not this great Babylon, that I have built for a royal dwelling by my mighty power and for the honor of my majesty?" Today we would call that spirit "humanism"— life where man is the center of the universe.

Is the city of Babylon actually going to be physically rebuilt? There are differences of opinion on that subject. Some say it will be rebuilt in Iraq, on or near its ancient location. I certainly don't have a problem believing that could happen. However, others believe it is not the city itself which is the focus in Revelation, but the spirit of the city, or the worldview. In that case, "Babylon" could be any of today's modern, world-class cities, all of which are centers of humanistic thought and action.

Wherever Babylon is located, we know the spirit of Babylon will be pervasive throughout the earth during the Great Tribulation. And by the end of that period, both the city and the spirit of Babylon will be destroyed.

THE REASONS FOR THE JUDGMENT OF BABYLON

The Apostle John saw an angel descending to earth whose splendor was so radiant it illuminated the entire earth (18:1). This angel pronounces judgment upon the city of Babylon. We saw judgment pronounced on Babylon ecclesiastically in chapter 17, and in this chapter we see Babylon destroyed commercially. The angel's repetition of "is fallen" is a reference to this two-fold judgment.

The word for "fallen" used here is a word that means to fall instantaneously. That is, the destruction of Babylon will not take place over a long period of time but will happen in a moment—actually, in one hour, we are told later in the chapter (verse 19). There are four reasons given for the destruction of Babylon.

Babylon Is Judged Because of Her Iniquity

In verse 5 we are told that Babylon's sins "have reached unto heaven, and God has remembered her iniquities." The verb for "reach," *kollao*, means to glue or weld together, meaning that Babylon's sins have been stacked one upon another like building blocks until they have reached heaven, God's domain. This is an obvious reference to the building of the Tower of Babel in Babylon (Genesis 11).

The city has become the habitation of every sort of unclean spirit and demonic power. While the original Babylon was inhabited by literal wild animals when she was destroyed (Isaiah 13:21-22), this reference in Revelation refers to the Satanic, demonic forces which will characterize Babylon under the rule of the Antichrist. Babylon will be the epitome of depravity in the last days. Everything in Babylon is carried out under the direction and influence of Satan and his demons.

Babylon is Judged Because of Her Influence

Verse 3 describes a city that not only is wicked and evil herself but has influenced others to follow her way of life. "The kings of the earth" have been seduced by Babylon's riches

> *The robber barons of the end times will exceed all of the excesses of Cornelius Vanderbilt, once America's richest man. He amassed more money in his personal coffers than was held in the U.S. Treasury.*
>
> *David Jeremiah*
> **Escape the Coming Night**

and have sold out themselves to her charms. The nations of the earth will come under the allure of Babylon's social, political, cultural and commercial life. Wanting to gain those same "riches" for themselves they will "drink of her wine" and fall into the trap of her world-view. Materialism and humanism will be the hallmarks of this system. Commercial advantage and gain will be the god of the nations as they come under Babylon's sway.

Babylon Is Judged Because of Her Infidelity

In verse 7, Babylon's words indicate that she considers herself immortal and invincible. She lives in iniquity and boasts of it, having no fear of anyone who might hold her accountable. Her words remind us of Satan's when he boasted that he would become like the most high God (Isaiah 14:14). Babylon is judged because of her spiritual infidelity, setting herself up as the ruler of the earth under the authority of Antichrist.

Babylon Is Judged Because of Her Inhumanity

In verses 12 and 13, 28 articles of merchandise are mentioned. First are articles which have first place in men's hearts, gold, silver, precious stones. Next come articles for show and adornment, then articles of precious wood, metal and ivory. Perfumes and other luxuries which speak of material indulgence are followed by more useful items such as horses and chariot. All of these items fall in the range of luxury items, things not necessarily needed for daily living. So Babylon is characterized by the pursuit of luxury.

Last in the list are the "bodies and souls of men," indicating that mankind will become nothing more than a commodity in the last days. In the Antichrist's economic system human beings will be dehumanized, which is what happens when God is taken out of the equation. When God is rejected, the image of God has no point of reference in the world.

THE REALITY OF THE JUDGMENT OF BABYLON

The word "anymore" is used as a negative six times in verses 21-23. It is the strongest way the Greek language could say, "not at all," and signifies the finality of the judgment of Babylon. No more will music fill the streets. No more will craftsmen work their trades. No more will the wheels of commerce turn. No more shall brides and grooms join themselves together. The city characterized by boisterous materialism, indulgence, and commerce will fall silent. There will be no one to purchase her wares. In one hour the sounds of worldly humanism will be silenced.

THE REACTIONS TO THE JUDGEMENTS OF BABYLON

The Monarchs of the Earth Will Mourn

Verses 9 and 10 describe the reactions of the kings of the earth who invested themselves and their nations in the worldliness of Babylon. They will wail and lament the destruction of the one in whom they had put their hope. The city and worldview they thought was their salvation will be destroyed and with it their hopes of continued indulgence and prosperity.

The Merchants of the Earth Will Mourn

Verses 11-17a contain lists of all the kinds of merchandise which will no longer be bought and sold around the world.

> *The angel's words announce most impressively the vanishing forever of all the joys and delights of the great city, the music and the song, the hum of industry, the brightness of its illumination, and, above all, the rejoicings of the bride and bridegroom, which in the Bible stand for the highest of all human joys.*
>
> Donald Grey Barnhouse

The economic hub of the world has spun off its axle, grinding the Antichrist's world system to a halt. Every kind of necessity and luxury will become unavailable. A world financial and economic crisis will result in the failure of banks and stock exchanges around the world. The merchants of the earth will mourn.

The Mariners Will Mourn

When the goods of the world are no longer bought and sold, those who in John's day delivered those goods across the seas mourn their own doom (verses 17-19). They are filled with terror as they watch the destruction of Babylon.

THE REJOICING OVER THE JUDGMENT OF BABYLON

Three classes of men on earth mourn the destruction of Babylon: kings, merchants, and mariners. But in heaven, three other classes of people rejoice over the destruction of Babylon: saints, apostles, and prophets. Unrestrained jubilation breaks forth as the people of God are at last vindicated and retribution is meted out upon the city which persecuted and martyred them (verses 20, 24).

A strong angel hurls a great stone, like a millstone, into the sea as a symbol of the violent destruction of Babylon (verse 21). It is as if the warning Jesus gave in Matthew 18:6 is carried out against Babylon. This city which caused so many in the world to stumble has a figurative millstone placed around her neck before she is cast into the sea of God's judgment.

"It is the first time in this book of tears that the command to rejoice is given. The saints are in Heaven from the time of the fourth chapter, and there is worship, and honor and glory and power given by them to God who is indeed worthy to receive this praise. But here—as though the saints now had their eyes adjusted to the glories of Heaven—the command of rejoicing is given. The saints are called to look down upon the world they have left. They see that the vile Babylon against which they have struggled and which poured out its scorn upon them, has come to a complete and final doom, and they know that this world-system will never rise again. There is full cause for rejoicing."[1]

Our Response to the Judgment of Babylon

How should we respond to the judgment and fall of Babylon? The voice John hears from heaven says it plainly:

> And I heard another voice from heaven saying, "Come out of her, my people, lest you share in her sins, and lest you receive of her plagues. For her sins have reached to heaven, and God has remembered her iniquities. Render to her just as she rendered to you, and repay her double according to her works; in the cup which she has mixed, mix double for her. In the measure that she glorified herself and lived luxuriously, in the same measure give her torment and sorrow; for she says in her heart, 'I sit as queen, and am no widow, and will not see sorrow.'" (18:4-7)

The command for the people of God to separate themselves from the world is a frequent one in Scripture. One of the best known exhortations to that effect is given by the Apostle Paul to the Corinthians in 2 Corinthians 6:14-18 where he tells them not to be unequally yoked with unbelievers. "Come out from among them and be separate" is the command.

There are two reasons for fleeing from Babylon. The first is to be separate from the sins of Babylon. Judgment is coming upon the world system of Satan, and, if we are separate from Babylon's sins, that judgment will not fall upon us. The second reason to flee is to escape the plagues and judgments coming upon the Antichrist and those who follow him.

Don't think that because literal Babylon lies in ruins today that the spirit of Babylon is not alive and well. Staying separate from that worldly spirit is a key to safety in the days ahead.

APPLICATION

1. Read James 4:13-17.

   a. How often do you make plans like those represented in verse 13?

   b. What does James say is wrong with that way of thinking? (verse 14)

   c. Why is there no contradiction between the "nobility" of man and the way James describes him in verse 14b? What is his point?

d. How should a Christian approach every day? (verse 15)

e. When we leave God out of our lives, in what are we actually boasting? (verse 16)

f. Why is it a sin to leave God out of our lives? (verse 17)

g. How could the attitude expressed in verse 13 be called the "spirit of Babylon"?

h. What must a Christian do to guard against the influences of "Babylon" in the world?

i. How does 1 John 2:18 give evidence that the spirit of living without God has already begun to influence the world?

2. Read James 5:1-6.
   a. Why is John taking the rich to task? (verses 4-6)

   b. The rich had not paid their obligations even though they had money. How does their money testify against them? (verse 3)

c. Which is more important—paying the people who have worked for us or hoarding up more wealth?

d. When we fail to honor and respect other people, what have we turned them into?

e. How is the dehumanizing of people a sign of the influence of the Antichrist, of the "spirit of Babylon"?

f. What does James say will come upon those who dehumanize others? (verse 1)

g. Is there anyone whom you are failing to treat with all due respect? How is that an evidence of an anti-God way of thinking in this world?

3. Read 1 Timothy 6:6-10.
   a. What is "godliness with contentment"? (verse 6)

   b. Why does it bring "great gain"?

c. What is the kind of gain the world entices people to pursue? (verse 9)

d. Why is the pursuit of monetary gain for its own sake a foolish endeavor? (verse 7)

e. How are the people described in verse 10b like the kings and nations who will be seduced by the wealth of Babylon in the Great Tribulation?

SPEAKING OF THE FUTURE . . .

A marvelous invention of the early twentieth century was the stereogram. It created a three-dimensional picture from viewing two, two-dimensional pictures through a stereoscopic viewer. Insert a card on which appeared two similar pictures, look through the viewer, and a three-dimensional image appeared.

Daniel, chapter seven, gives a sort of stereoscopic view of the heavens and the earth all at the same time. On the one hand, we see great turmoil and unrest on earth as kingdoms collide with one another. On the other hand, a look into heaven reveals God, the Ancient of Days, ruling sovereignly from His throne. Both images combine to give an accurate picture of the universe. Jesus Christ came from heaven to bring "peace on earth." For the first time since the Garden of Eden, it became possible for the sovereign peace of heaven to replace the turmoil of earth in the hearts of men. Our challenge is to allow the Ancient of Days to take His rightful place upon the throne of our hearts.

Are you a stereoscopic image of life in this world—living with peace in the midst of turmoil and trouble?

> HOLY, HOLY, HOLY, LORD GOD ALMIGHTY,
> WHO WAS AND IS AND IS TO COME!
> —The four living creatures at the
> throne of God in Revelation 4:8

Note:

[1] Donald Grey Barnhouse, *Revelation: An Expository Commentary* (Grand Rapids: Zondervan, 1971), 221–222.

THE MARRIAGE SUPPER OF THE LAMB

Revelation 19:1-10

In this lesson we get a glimpse of the wedding and marriage supper of the Lamb.

You will find more in-depth information on this lesson in the book *Escape the Coming Night*, chapter 17, pages 217-222.

OUTLINE

With all the tumultuous and dark events taking place in the last few years of the Tribulation, the reader of Revelation longs for relief—a ray of celebration in the midst of judgment. It comes at the end of the Tribulation when heaven rejoices over God's victory and the marriage of His Son.

I. **The Celebration in Heaven**
   A. The Hallelujah for the Salvation of God
   B. The Hallelujah for the Severity of God
   C. The Hallelujah of the Sovereignty of God
   D. The Hallelujah for the Supremacy of God

II. **The Ceremony**
   A. The Sacred Wedding
   B. The Supper Meal

W ith this lesson and our study of Revelation 19 we make a sudden turn in the "tone" of what we have studied thus far. Chapter 19 stands in sharp contrast to the content of the previous 18 chapters. The destruction of Babylon, the capital of the Antichrist's world empire, marks the end of the Great Tribulation. The horrors, which have filled the earth through the judgments God has poured out and through the demonically orchestrated actions of the Beast, have all been stilled. Darkness gives way to light, and sobbing is about to give way to song. The most anticipated event in history is about to take place— the Second Coming of Jesus Christ. That event forms the bridge between the gory days of the Great Tribulation and the glory days of the Millennial Kingdom.

The first ten verses of chapter 10 describe two events that take place in heaven at the end of the Tribulation: a celebration and a ceremony—both involving the Bride of Christ, the Church.

THE CELEBRATION IN HEAVEN

The multitude in heaven says, "Alleluia!" in praise to the Lord for what has been revealed about Him throughout the Great Tribulation. "Alleluia" is the Greek version of the Hebrew *Hallelujah,* a word which meant "praise ye the Lord." It is found only four times in the New Testament while occurring often in the Old—usually translated into English as "Praise the Lord!"

The Hallelujah for the Salvation of God

Some of the words in Handel's great "Hallelujah Chorus" come from the first six verses of Revelation 19. Indeed, some have called this section of Scripture the New Testament's "Hallelujah Chorus." God is praised in heaven for one simple reason. Those praising God are there because God provided their redemption. God has personally saved every person who makes it from earth to heaven, and He is worthy to be praised for that reason.

The Hallelujah for the Severity of God

Why would anyone rejoice and praise God for His severity? It is because of how and against whom His severity was directed. The destruction of Babylon, the world-controlling religious and economic system, has just occurred. Looking down from heaven, the saints see that these anti-God systems of thought and practice have been destroyed and eliminated from earth. It is for that reason they rejoice. They know God's judgments are "true and righteous" and that He judged the "great harlot who corrupted the earth with her fornication" (19:2). His severity also brought about vengeance for those who were martyred by the Beast.

The smoke from the destruction of Babylon going up "forever and ever" (19:3) is evidence that, even in the face of judgment, those at enmity with God do not repent and change their minds. I am continually surprised, as I study the Book of Revelation, at the hardness of heart of the impenitent sinner. No matter what judgment God brings, or what mercy He extends, the carnal sinner continues to rebel against God. God's judgment is praiseworthy because it is just.

> *So long as the Godhead is to endure and so long as the believers are to reign with Him in glory, so long must the wrath of God be poured upon those who know not God and obey not the Gospel of our Lord Jesus Christ. There is not the shadow of evidence in the Bible that the lake of fire will ever turn one heart toward God or cause one guilty sinner to relax in the slightest the enmity against God that characterizes the carnal mind.*
>
> *Dr. John Walvoord*

The Hallelujah of the Sovereignty of God

The key word in this third reason for rejoicing in heaven is "Amen" (19:4). This is a word of sacred ratification in Scripture, a word of sealing and of affirmation. When the 24 elders and the four cherubim say, "Amen! Alleluia!" they are giving consent and affirmation to an act of judgment that they know to be righteous and true. "Amen" and "Hallelujah" are not English words; rather they are transliterations of Hebrew words which are pronounced the same in every language. Believers from around the world who do not speak each other's language can establish instant fellowship and communion when they share an "Amen" and "Hallelujah" together. When heaven and earth agree by saying "Amen!" to God's acts, it is an affirmation of His sovereignty over all things.

The Hallelujah for the Supremacy of God

Verses 5 and 6, while the last of the words of praise offered to God, are actually a prelude to the wedding ceremony that is about to take place. They are both a conclusion to the acknowledgement that God has acted sovereignly in judgment upon sin on earth and an introduction to His sovereignty in saving a multitude from earth who will be united forever with His Son. It is like the music we listen to in the hour just before a wedding ceremony takes place, music which speaks of the greatness of the ceremony we are about to witness.

THE CEREMONY

An invitation is issued to the marriage supper of the Lamb in verses 7-9. This is the event which all true believers should be anticipating more than any other—the moment in which they become one with their Savior, where the bride of Christ and the Head of the Church are united.

Understanding the rituals of a Jewish wedding ceremony will help us understand the marriage supper of the Lamb. There were three major steps in the pattern of marriage in the ancient Near East. Step one was the legal marriage, often consummated by the parents of the bride and bridegroom. This involved the payment of a dowry and resulted in a legal marriage. Often it was accomplished solely by the parents without the bride and groom having met one another. Secondly, after the legal marriage, the groom (with his friends) would go to the house of the bride and "claim" the bride for himself, taking her back to his own house. The final stage of the wedding was the bridal procession followed by a marriage feast which would often last for several days.

Following this outline, we can see clear parallels in our relationship with the Lord. First, the legal marriage takes place at the time of our conversion to Christ—positionally, we are already united with Him by faith. As the bride of Christ, we are now awaiting the time when the groom will come to claim us for Himself and take us back to His own mansion which He has been preparing for us (John 14:2). Finally, the marriage supper of the Lamb takes place after we have been taken to be with the Groom. It is that marriage supper in heaven which verse 7 declares is now ready.

When reading the account in Revelation of the marriage supper, it is important to understand the relative importance of the groom to the bride. In modern weddings, all attention is focused on the bride, but in Oriental weddings the opposite was true. The groom was the central figure. We are reading about the marriage supper of the Lamb, not the marriage supper of the bride or even the couple. The Lamb of God is the central figure in this marriage and marriage supper.

The Sacred Wedding

This refers to the second of the three steps outlined above in the ancient pattern for marriage, the coming of the bridegroom to claim the bride for his own. This is fulfilled, of course, at the Rapture of the church. We anticipate the day when the Lord Jesus Christ will return for us, His bride, and take us to be with Himself. Prior to that event, though legally married, we are still in an engagement period, as Paul expressed in 2 Corinthians 11:2: "I have betrothed you to one husband, that I may present you as a chaste virgin to Christ." The church at present is engaged to Christ, waiting on the day when He returns to claim us as His own.

Scripture does not tell us exactly when the marriage takes place in heaven, but it would appear to happen in this order: Rapture, judgment seat of Christ, marriage ceremony, marriage supper, second coming of Christ. The Rapture and second coming are the "bookends" on the seven-year Tribulation period, so the marriage ceremony and supper take place during that time. We know the marriage ceremony takes place after the judgment seat of Christ because of verses 7 and 8: The bride has made herself ready and she is arrayed in clean and bright linen which is the righteous acts of the saints. We know from 1 Corinthians 3 that the unrighteous works of the saints are burned up with fire at the judgment seat of Christ, so that only righteous deeds remain. If the Church appears clothed in fine linen, which is her righteous

> *The wedding gown will be made by the master Designer, and it symbolizes the righteous deeds done by the bride on earth. . . .*
>
> *The lavishness or drabness of that wedding gown will be determined by a report on the deeds performed on earth in the Spirit, not in the flesh.*
>
> *How we use the gifts God gave us on earth will decide the way we are presented to the Bridegroom when He comes. Will we be dressed shabbily or lavishly?*
>
> *David Jeremiah*
> *Escape the Coming Night*

deeds, it is because she has already passed before the judgment seat of Christ.

The most important person at the wedding is the Bridegroom, who is here referred to as "the Lamb" (19:7). Why does Christ come to this wedding ceremony as "the Lamb" instead of any of the 700 other titles by which He is referred to in Scripture? From our perspective as the bride of Christ, I think I know why He comes to the wedding as "the Lamb." I think it is because we fell in love with the Lamb. While we honor Him as King, Creator, Servant, and all the other titles of which He is deserving, we were saved by Him as the Lamb, the Lamb of God who takes away the sin of the world.

The Supper Meal

The marriage supper is mentioned in verse 9. There is some detail which we need to note concerning the location of the supper. While the wedding ceremony itself appears to take place in heaven, the marriage supper seems to be held on earth.

After the wedding ceremony, the Lord returns to earth with His bride at the Second Coming. Since verse 9 says, "Blessed are those who are called to the marriage supper," it is obvious that there are more than just the bride and Bridegroom at the supper. The Bridegroom is Christ and the bride is the Church. So who are the others? John the Baptist gives us a clue in John 3 when he speaks of the "friend" of the groom, who in that passage has to be Israel. Therefore, it would appear that the marriage supper of the Lamb is held on earth so that the redeemed of Israel, who have gone through the Tribulation and survived the persecutions of the Antichrist, may attend and rejoice at the marriage supper. So the marriage supper of the Lamb will be a magnificent redemptive meal celebrating the uniting of Jews and Gentiles into one body, married to the Head of the Body, Jesus Christ. The fact that it takes place on earth is a prelude to the thousand years the Bridegroom and Bride will spend reigning over the earth during the Millennium. The time of our preparation and purification is almost over. The day of the marriage ceremony is close at hand.

The Old Testament story of Abraham's preparation of a bride for Isaac is instructive regarding our marriage to the Lamb (Genesis 24). Abraham is a picture of God the Father, Isaac a picture of Christ, Abraham's servant Eleazar a picture of the Holy Spirit, and Rebekah a picture of the Christian. Just as Abraham sent Eleazar to a foreign land to seek out a bride for Isaac, so the Holy Spirit has been moving throughout the earth seeking out the Bride of Christ. Every time someone is saved, the Bride's identity becomes more complete. As Isaac went to meet Rebekah when he saw Eleazar approaching, so Christ descends to meet His Bride. As Eleazar and Isaac took Rebekah to meet Abraham, so the Church will be taken before the Father in order for the ceremony and the supper to take place.

The Father has sent the Spirit into the world to call out a bride for His only Son. The bride (the Church) has been legally transferred from her former domain to the domain of the Father; her citizenship is now in heaven. Meanwhile, the Son is preparing a heavenly home for His bride. He will return to take His bride to Himself, and join with her in a ceremony in heaven and a feast on earth among the friends of the Son. What a beautiful picture! If the Bridegroom comes tonight to meet His bride and take her to meet the Father, will you be among those taken? Don't let another day go by without being sure you are part of the bride of the Lamb.

APPLICATION

1. In addition to the Bridegroom and Bride, identify the other metaphors used to portray the relationship between Christ and the Church.

   a. John 10:1-18

   b. John 15:5

   c. Ephesians 2:20b-22

   d. Hebrews 4:14; 1 Peter 2:5, 9

c. Ephesians 5:23, 30

2. Read Psalm 45 as a figurative representation of a conquering king and his marriage celebration.

a. This song is in praise of a Hebrew king, probably a descendant of David. How could it also be speaking figuratively of Christ? (verse 2)

b. What part of Christ's future role is pictured in verse 3? (Revelation 19:11-16)

c. Compare verse 5 with Revelation 19:17-18.

d. How does the writer of Hebrews apply verse 6-7?
(Hebrews 1:8-9)

e. How is the beauty of the king/groom portrayed? (verse 8)

f. Compare the bride's stature in verse 9b with the church in
Ephesians 5:27.

g. How would you apply the groom's attitude toward the bride in verse 11 with Christ's love for the Church? (Ephesians 5:25-26).

h. How do the "the virgins, her companions" speak of the purity of those who have kept themselves pure from Babylon during the Tribulation? (Revelation 17:5)

i. Compare verse 15 with John 14:2-3.

j. How is verse 17 a picture of the ultimate state of peace on earth? (Revelation 21:24, 26; 22:2)

3. How do the two contrasting sentiments of punishment and praise in Psalm 104:35 foreshadow the celebration in heaven at the end of the Tribulation?

SPEAKING OF THE FUTURE . . .

Ray Boltz tells a story in song of a father and two small sons who journey to Jerusalem at Passover. The father tells his sons to "watch the lamb" when he is pressed into service by a Roman soldier to carry the cross of a man sentenced to die on Golgotha. Finding their father at the foot of the cross, the boys cry because their lamb has run away. Answering their questions about the man who has been crucified, the father only says, "Watch the Lamb."

"Watch the Lamb" is a beautiful retelling of the mystery of Jesus, the Lamb of God who takes away the sins of the world. Called "the Lamb of God" by John the Baptist, Jesus Christ was known to John at their first meeting as the sacrifice God had sent into the world to atone for man's sin. Reference to the Lamb is absent in the rest of the New Testament—until heaven's curtain is pulled back in Revelation. There, Christ as the Lamb is mentioned 26 times. He is the focal point of worship in heaven for having been slain to take away the sin of the world. He is the sacrifice for sin for all who believe in Him.

Are your eyes on the Lamb? If He has taken away your sin, prepare to join heaven's choir by singing His praise on earth today.

> BEHOLD, THE LION OF THE TRIBE OF JUDAH,
> THE ROOT OF DAVID, HAS PREVAILED . . . .
> —An elder in heaven in Revelation 5:5

THE SECOND COMING OF CHRIST

Revelation 19:11-21

*In this lesson we see the King of Kings
victorious at Armageddon.*

You will find more in-depth information on this lesson in the
book *Escape the Coming Night,* chapter 17, pages 223-227.

OUTLINE

"Armageddon" is one of those Biblical words that has been
absorbed into the language of many cultures. Used often, it
is rarely used in its Biblical context. Unfortunately, many will
discover too late that Armageddon is going to be the worst
conflagration ever visited upon planet earth.

   I.   **The Advent of Christ**

  II.   **The Armies of Christ**

 III.   **The Authority of Christ**

  IV.   **The Avenging of Christ**
        A. The Fowls of Heaven
        B. The Foes of Heaven

S tarting in Revelation 4, we have seen planet earth ruined by men and ruled by Satan, but in this lesson we will see the world reclaimed by Jesus Christ. The Bible tells us we are not to know the date of the return of Christ, only that we are to know for a certainty that it is going to happen. The only "when" we know is that it will be seven years after the Rapture of the Church. The Rapture starts the end time prophetic clock ticking, but since we don't know the date of that event we don't know the dates of the events dependent on it.

The Bible is filled with references to the second coming of Christ—1,845 references in all. It is emphasized in 17 Old Testament books, and 70 percent of the chapters of the New Testament make reference to it. Christ Himself said He would return, as did angels who spoke to the apostles at Christ's ascension into heaven. This abundance of evidence does not keep scoffers from asking, "Where is the promise of His coming?" (2 Peter 3:4). That question is answered in Revelation 19:11-16— and forms the focus of our study in this lesson.

If the Bible makes anything clear it is that the second coming of Christ will be a glorious event which all the world will witness, believers and unbelievers alike. Christ said His coming would be like the lightning that begins in the east and shines to the west, illuminating the whole of the heavens (Matthew 24:27). His coming will illumine the dark days at the end of the Tribulation like lightning illumines the pitch-black darkness of a violent thunderstorm. Riding on a white horse in the midst of that lightning will be found the King of Kings Himself accompanied by all the saints.

THE ADVENT OF CHRIST (19:11-13)

The fact that John sees the door of heaven open here is significant. The first time it was opened was in Revelation 4:1, so the Church might enter heaven at the Rapture. We have no mention of the door opening since. Now it is opened for a second time, so the saints can return to earth accompanying their Lord. It opens first for the Rapture and secondly for the revelation. And by way of review . . . the Rapture is that event which we are waiting for at the present time, when the Church is taken from earth to be with the Lord during the period of the seven-year Tribulation.

The revelation of Jesus Christ, however, is when He is revealed in all His glory to come and destroy the enemies of God at Armageddon and set up the kingdom of God on earth. There are some notable differences between the two events:

- Rapture: Christ comes *for* His saints.
- Revelation: Christ comes *with* His saints.

- Rapture: the church meets Jesus in the air.
- Revelation: Jesus descends to earth, to the Mount of Olives.

- Rapture: coming of the Lord with blessing in mind.
- Revelation: coming of the Lord with judgment in mind.

- Rapture: imminent.
- Revelation: always no less than seven years away (from the Rapture).

Verse 11 tells us a name which Christ is called, "Faithful and True," one of three in this chapter (the others being "Word of God" and "King of Kings and Lord of Lords"). Besides His names, the attributes represented by His appearance and clothing are important as well. His eyes are flames of fire (1:14; 2:18) which burn up all that is false as He gazes upon the hearts and minds of mankind. His many crowns speak of His sovereignty, that no one is above Him in rule. His robe dipped in blood speaks of the redemption He secured for us on the cross as the Lamb that was slain. For all eternity we will celebrate the shed blood which brought about our redemption from the penalty of sin.

> *In these three names [the ones in Revelation 19], the Word of God has encompassed the entire ministry of the Lord Jesus Christ. His eternity in the past, His incarnation when He walked upon this earth, and His sovereign coming as King of Kings and Lord of Lords.*
>
> Dr. Harry Ironside

Revelation 1:7 says that "every eye will see Him, even they who pierced Him." People have asked me how this could possibly take place. In today's technological world it does not seem hard to figure out, with satellite and cable television all over the world. But some do not believe it has anything to do with that. Rather it will simply be His glory that will be visible from anywhere on earth. Somehow, through technology or the radiance of His glory, all the world will know that Jesus has returned. But He does not return alone.

THE ARMIES OF CHRIST (19:14)

The Bible says when Christ returns He will bring with Him an army. Every believer who died before the Rapture, or went up to be with the Lord at the Rapture, will return with Him. The purpose of our coming with Him is to help execute judgment upon those who have denied Christ during the Tribulation (Jude 14-15). The 144,000 witness preached to them, God's two faithful witnesses preached to them, and plenty of Bibles and Christian literature were around by which to discover the truth, but they did not. And with the return of Christ and His armies, judgment will come (see also 2 Thessalonians 1:7-10).

Note the word in verse 14 is "armies"—plural. It is not the "army" of heaven but the "armies." We do not know exactly the significance of that, but it could represent Old Testament saints, New Testament saints, and Tribulation saints all combined in one giant "army" of the Lord. More important than who they are is how they are dressed. These armies go into battle dressed in pure white garments, strange from a military perspective. The reason is that they will not go into battle to fight like our modern soldiers do. In fact, they will be spectators who watch the Battle of Armageddon end simply by the words coming from Jesus' mouth.

THE AUTHORITY OF CHRIST (19:15-16)

In Revelation 1:16 we read about the "sharp two-edged sword" coming from Christ's mouth as He was prepared to levy judgment upon the seven churches. Here, on the way to further judgment, we see Him again with a sword coming out of His mouth. This sword does not represent the Word of God (Ephesians 6:17). Rather, "sword" is used symbolically to represent a sharp instrument of war with which Christ will smite the nations and establish His absolute rule. The rod of iron denotes absolute sovereignty in His reign as King of Kings (Psalm 2:9; Revelation 2:27).

As Christ leads forth His armies in victory, John sees a name written on His thigh, "KING OF KINGS AND LORD OF LORDS." We are familiar with this double name, but now is the time it takes on its intended significance. Of all the kings on earth, He is the King. Of all earthly lords (rulers, those in authority), He is the Lord. Every knee will bow before Him when He comes to earth (Isaiah 45:23; Romans 14:11; Philippians 2:10-11). He will fulfill the wonderful prophecy we review every Christmas, "the government will be upon His shoulder" (Isaiah 9:6).

THE AVENGING OF CHRIST (19:17-21)

The vengeance Christ brings upon the enemies of God is presented in an unusual way in verses 17-21. The fowls of heaven and the foes of heaven are the two metaphors John uses to convey what will happen when Christ comes.

The Fowls of Heaven

In his vision John sees an angel, standing in the sun, crying out with a loud voice to all the birds of heaven to gather for a great feast. There is a terrible sense of foreboding as these birds of prey are called to come and clean up the flesh of the mighty men who will be killed in the Battle of Armageddon. The word for "birds" is the word *orneois* which is literally translated as "vulture." All the vultures of earth are invited to come and feast on the carcasses of those who fall before the sword of the Lord. Notice that those who fall in battle are the "mighty men" of earth, the captains and kings, along with "the flesh of all people, free and slave, both small and great" (19:18).

I hope you have noticed there are two suppers in Revelation 19. There is the Marriage Supper of the Lamb and there is "the supper of the great God" (19:17). The former is a time of great rejoicing and celebration while the latter is a time of wailing and lament as those who fall in the battle against Christ are consumed. Someone has said we get to take our choice of which supper to attend. Those who choose to put their trust for eternity in Christ will attend the Marriage Supper of the Lamb. But those who reject His Gospel, His invitation of love and grace, and who survive the Tribulation period, will attend the supper of the great God. You would not eat the food, but you would be the food—food for the vultures of heaven which will come to clean up the remains of the battle. And they apparently go away satisfied (19:21).

The Foes of Heaven

It is amazing here, as well as all throughout the Book of Revelation, that mankind continues to gather together to make a stand against the God who created him. But the Antichrist and the kings of the earth and the pitiful souls following them into battle gather together one last time to try to defeat Jesus Christ. Their army will be made up of the kings and soldiers of the 10 nations of the revived Roman Empire, as well as the Beast and False Prophet. The Antichrist leads the way in defying Christ's authority and right to rule—the ultimate in rebellion against God. All the rebellion of the prior seven years comes to a head at the Mountain of Megiddo, the battle of Armageddon. The degree of judgment meted out will be directly comparable to the degree of rebellion the Antichrist has fomented during the Tribulation period. His judgment will be terrible because His acts have been terrible.

The battle is joined in verse 20 and immediately the Beast and the False Prophet are "captured." This word is very interesting, providing a picture of the Lord reaching out and snatching them—grabbing them by the scruff of the neck, as we might say in our modern language.

> *Two men be it noted are taken alive. They are the two arch-conspirators who have both sold largely in [Revelation]. The Beast and the False Prophet, the civil and religious leaders of the last League of Nations, which will be Satan-inspired in its origin, and Satan-directed until its doom. These two men are cast alive in the Lake of Fire, burning with fire and brimstone, where, a thousand years later, they are still said to be suffering the vengeance of eternal fire. Thus incidentally proving that the Lake of Fire is not annihilation and that it is not purgatorial either, for it neither annihilates or purifies these two fallen foes of God and man after a thousand years under its judgment.*
>
> *Dr. Harry Ironside*

It is as if the Lord has had enough of their rebellion and puts an end to it immediately once the battle begins. And their fate is as infamous as their deeds. They become the first two residents of hell: "These two were cast alive into the lake of fire burning with brimstone" (19:20). People who die rejecting the Lord do not go straight to hell; they go to a place known as Hades. But the Beast and False Prophet go straight to hell, even before Satan, who does not arrive until the end of the thousand-year millennium. When he arrives there, the Beast and False Prophet are still there, where "they will be tormented day and night forever and ever" (20:10).

It would be wrong for us to be callous or casual about the horrific events in store for many of our fellow human beings. As we watch for His appearing we should live with a careful attitude toward our own lives and a compassionate attitude toward those who don't know Christ. Here are 10 things the Word of God says we should do to maintain purity and holiness:

1. Refrain from judging others (1 Corinthians 4:5).

2. Remember the Lord's table (1 Corinthians 11:26).

3. Respond to life spiritually (Colossians 3:1-4).

4. Relate to one another in love (1 Thessalonians 3:12-13).

5. Restore the bereaved (1 Thessalonians 4:13-18).

6. Recommit ourselves to the ministry (2 Timothy 4:1-2).

7. Refuse to neglect church (Hebrews 10:24-25).

8. Remain steadfast (James 5:7-8).

9. Renounce sin in our lives (1 John 2:28-29).

10. Reach the lost (Jude 21-23).

Have you made your choice as to which banquet you want to attend? There's an eternity of difference between being invited to supper and being had for supper. I know for a certainty which supper I plan to attend and which one I plan to avoid. I hope you do as well.

APPLICATION

1. Read Zechariah 14:1-9

   a. What period in Israel's history does the prophet seem to be addressing? (verses 1-2)

   b. What is described in verses 3, 4, and 9 that did not happen in the Old Testament?

   c. In light of verse 9, what period of time is the prophet also seeing in his overlapping prophecy?

d. What does he see happening to the Mount of Olives? (verse 4)

e. How does verse 5b parallel with Revelation 19:14?

f. Consistent with previous events during the Tribulation, what will happen in the heavens on that day? (verse 6)

g. In light of John 7:37-39, how would you interpret verse 8?

h. How does "'The LORD is one,' And His name one" compare to the phrase of "Lord of Lords"? (verse 9; Revelation 19:16)

2. Read Matthew 24:27-31.

    a. What will be the reaction of the nations of earth when the Son of Man appears in the sky? (verse 30)

    b. Is verse 31 describing the Rapture of the church or the Second Coming? Why?

3. Read Acts 1:1-12.

   a. What is the context of this setting? (verse 3)

   b. What command did Christ give the apostles? (verse 4)

   c. What were they most interested in knowing? (verse 6)

d. What do you think they meant by this question?

e. What was Jesus' answer to them? (verse 7)

f. Could Jesus have told them "when" even if He wanted to? Why or why not? (Matthew 24:36)

SPEAKING OF THE FUTURE . . .

There you are watching your family's favorite nature program. The cameras are recording the great lions on Africa's Serengeti Plain as they stalk their prey. Slinking silently through the tall grass, a lioness suddenly springs forward and plants her sharp teeth in a vice-like grip on her helpless meal—a bale of hay. After thrashing it around for good measure, she settles in for a relaxing vegetarian meal.

What? If you actually saw this, you'd think it was a joke. But a day is coming when it will be the norm. All the violence on planet earth will be subdued when the Prince of Peace comes to reign— even violence in the animal kingdom. The prophet Isaiah foretold this reality saying, "the lion shall eat straw like the ox" (Isaiah 11:7). This is simply a return to the divinely established pattern of the Garden of Eden (Genesis 1:30)—a pattern interrupted when all of creation was tainted by sin. Though violence covers the earth— and may have touched you—it is only for a season. A great harvest of peace is just over the divine horizon.

Animals may have to wait to experience peace, but we can have it today in Jesus.

THEY SHALL NOT HURT NOR DESTROY IN ALL MY HOLY MOUNTAIN,
FOR THE EARTH SHALL BE FULL OF THE KNOWLEDGE OF THE LORD
AS THE WATERS COVER THE SEA.

—Isaiah in Isaiah 11:9

THE THOUSAND YEAR REIGN OF CHRIST

Revelation 20:1-10

In this lesson we learn about the long-promised reign of God on earth.

You will find more in-depth information on this lesson in the book *Escape the Coming Night*, chapter 18, pages 229-234.

OUTLINE

If you are a fan of nature shows on TV, get ready for a change. During the millennium the peace of God will be so pervasive that lions will be stalking bales of hay instead of antelope. That's how world-changing the reign of Christ will be. And it will last for a thousand years!

   I.   The Kingdom Is Necessary to Reward the People of God

  II.   The Kingdom is Necessary to Respond
        to the Disciples' Prayer

 III.   The Kingdom Is Necessary to Redeem Creation

  IV.   The Kingdom Is Necessary to Reemphasize
        Man's Depravity

   V.   The Characteristics of the Millennium
        A. It Will Be a Time of Peace
        B. It Will Be a Time of Prosperity
        C. It Will Be a Time of Purity
        D. It Will Be a Time of Perpetual Health
        E. It Will Be a Time of Personal Joy

OVERVIEW

Some 250 years ago, a man by the name of Isaac Watts wrote a hymn based on Psalm 98 called "Joy to the World." We sing it at Christmas to celebrate Christ's first coming. Unfortunately, that is not what it is about. Watts wrote the hymn to celebrate the Kingship of Christ over all the earth, as the words indicate:

> Joy to the World! The Lord is come!
> Let earth receive her King.
> Let every heart prepare him room,
> And heaven and nature sing.
>
> No more let sins and sorrows grow,
> Nor thorns infest the ground;
> He comes to make his blessings flow
> Far as the curse is found.
>
> He rules the world with truth and grace;
> And makes the nations prove
> The glories of his righteousness,
> And the wonders of His love.

As far as I can tell, the nations have not proved the "glories of His righteousness." But a day is coming when they will.

Revelation 20 contains the only reference to the thousand year reign of Christ found in the New Testament, the Millennium ("millennium" = a thousand year period of time). Verse 4 says, "And they lived and reigned with Christ for a thousand years." In the first seven verses of chapter 20 John mentions the thousand year period no less than six times. Critics argue, that since 2 Peter 3:8 says a thousand years is like a day, that John can't mean a literal thousand year period. Some of the same folks who argue that way say the days of creation in Genesis 1 are not literal either, that they represent thousands of years of time. You cannot have it both ways. It is better just to let the Bible speak plainly for itself.

The kingdom in the Bible is referred to in many ways: "the kingdom of heaven," "the kingdom of God," "the kingdom of Christ," "times of refreshing," "the fullness of times," "the world to come." And John sees this period as a time when Satan is bound in the bottomless pit which allows for a period of peace on earth (20:2-3). John also saw a "first resurrection" which occurs just before the Millennium begins. This is the raising to life of those martyred for the Lord during the Tribulation who are resurrected and live during the Millennium. The unsaved dead are brought back to life in a "second resurrection" at the end of the Millennium when they are judged at the Great White Throne Judgment of God (20:11-15). At the end of the Millennium Satan will be released from the bottomless pit to lead a rebellion of "Gog and Magog" (20:8) against Christ and His rule. John outlines very clearly the details of what will happen in association with the thousand year rule of Christ.

To summarize what we have learned thus far, adding the Millennium to it, the next event on God's prophetic calendar is the Rapture of the Church. With the departure of the Church and the Spirit from earth, seven years of Tribulation begin, culminated by the Battle of Armageddon when Christ returns (the second coming of Christ) with the saints to defeat the Antichrist. Following this defeat, and the consigning of Satan to the bottomless pit for a thousand years, the Millennial reign of Christ begins.

> *The Jews of the Old Testament studied the Old Testament Scriptures and they were able to put together the kingdom age that we study here in [Revelation 20] without even having the New Testament. And they believed with all of their hearts that Christ was coming someday to set up His kingdom, that it would last for one thousand years.*
>
> *Rene Pache*

Abroad in Christendom today are three main views about the Millennium, the first two of which I believe to be erroneous.

1. Post-millennialism.

   Popularized in the early 20th century, when it looked like mankind was on his way to establishing peace on earth, this view teaches the second coming of Christ will occur "post" (after) the Millennium. That is, the church will expand and cover the earth and establish the kingdom of God, after which Christ will return and eternity will begin. This view has fallen out of favor simply because two world wars and other evidences of carnality and depravity have made it clear that man will not establish utopia on earth. Scripture nowhere teaches that everything is going to get better and better. In fact, it teaches the opposite. Very few supporters of post-millennialism can be found today.

2. Amillennialism.

   As with other words, an initial "a" is a negative, negating the concept of the word to which it is attached (e.g., an "amoral" person lacks morals). Therefore, the amillennialist does not believe there will be a millennium at all. Their main premise is that the idea of a millennial kingdom was taught by the Jewish prophets and that the church has become the fulfillment of the promises to the Jews. Therefore, the blessings of an earthly, millennial kingdom are being manifested spiritually in the Church of Jesus Christ today. When Isaiah 11:7 teaches that the cow and the bear will graze peacefully together and the lion will eat straw instead of other animals, the amillennialists say that means something—but they aren't sure what. The problem, of course, is, who sets themselves up as the standard to decide how the whole Old Testament should be re-interpreted now that the church has inherited the promises made to Israel? Amillennialism leads to a highly allegorical interpretation of Scripture.

3. Premillennialism.

   I believe this is the correct Biblical view. It teaches that the return of Christ will occur "pre" (before) a literal, earthly, thousand year period of peace on earth. Christ will reign over earth from the throne of His forefather king David from the city of Jerusalem. This is the oldest of the three views, having been held predominantly by the church fathers from the apostolic period forward. Premillennialism is based on a literal reading and interpreting of Scripture.

There are faithful evangelicals who hold to each of the three views, and one's view on the Millennium should never be a test of fellowship or orthodoxy. But it is important to establish a Scriptural foundation for one's views on the Millennium, which we will do in this lesson. There are a number of reasons why a literal, earthly kingdom is a necessity in the plan of God.

THE KINGDOM IS NECESSARY TO REWARD THE PEOPLE OF GOD

The Bible says that God intends to reward the faithful for their commitment, and the Millennium is one of those rewards. Believers will co-reign with Jesus Christ over all the earth. Many Scriptures attest to this fact: Isaiah 40:10; Matthew 5:12; 16:27;

25:34; Colossians 3:24; Revelation 22:12. One of the rewards of faithfulness to God during this life is the reward of rulership and authority during the kingdom. It will be interesting to see who is assigned to rule over whom during that period. Since rewards are given for the faithfulness and motivation of the heart, there will undoubtedly be some surprises.

THE KINGDOM IS NECESSARY TO RESPOND TO THE DISCIPLES' PRAYER

In Luke 11 and Matthew 6 we have the record of Jesus teaching the disciples to pray that the kingdom would come "on earth as it is in heaven." Has that prayer been answered yet? Not literally, though we do have Christ ruling in our hearts. But that is not what the prayer is about. The prayer is that the will and rule of God would fill the earth just as it fills heaven. Therefore, in order for the prayer of every person who has ever prayed the Lord's Prayer to be answered, the kingdom of God needs to come and cover the earth. That is the only way God's will will be done "on earth as it is in heaven."

THE KINGDOM IS NECESSARY TO REDEEM CREATION

In Genesis 3 God cursed the creation because of Adam's sin. From that point on, earth has groaned under the weight of that curse. While we may think the earth is beautiful today, what we see is just a shadow of what it was and what it will be again. *The Living Bible* paraphrase of Romans 8:19-22 says it well:

"For all creation is waiting patiently and hopefully for that future day when God will resurrect his children. For on that day, thorns and thistles, sin, death and decay, the things that overcame the world against its will, at God's command will all disappear, and the world around us will share in the glorious freedom from sin which God's children enjoy, for we know that even the things of nature, like animals and plants, suffer in sickness and death as they await this great event."

THE KINGDOM IS NECESSARY TO REEMPHASIZE MAN'S DEPRAVITY

All throughout Scripture man has demonstrated that, even in the best of circumstances, he cannot keep his depravity under control. The fallen human nature of man will not be eliminated until eternity begins at the end of the millennial kingdom. Even during the Millennium, when Jesus Christ Himself is ruling and reigning on earth, the depravity of man will manifest itself. Those faithful saints who survive the Tribulation period will, though redeemed, be fallen human beings just like you and me. They will "be fruitful and multiply" over all the earth for a thousand years, bearing children with fallen human natures like their parents. And according to Revelation 20:7-10, Satan will lead a rebellion of deceived human beings at the end of the Millennium. This final revolt will demonstrate in a final way that, apart from the intervention of God, man is totally incapable of righteousness on his own. God's judgment of man will once again, and for the final time, be vindicated.

> *Therefore with joy you will draw water from the wells of salvation. And in that day you will say: "Praise the LORD, call upon His name; declare His deeds among the peoples, make mention that His name is exalted. Sing to the LORD, for He has done excellent things; this is known in all the earth. Cry out and shout, O inhabitant of Zion, for great is the Holy One of Israel in your midst!"*
>
> *The Prophet Isaiah, 12:4-6*

THE CHARACTERISTICS OF THE MILLENNIUM

While the Millennium will be characterized by countless numbers of blessings and benefits, five major categories are clearly emphasized in Scripture.

It Will Be a Time of Peace

The prophet Micah in the Old Testament gives one of the clearest statements about the reign of the Messiah (4:2-3). In essence, there will be no more war. Military implements will be re-tooled for agricultural use and nations will not lift up the sword against each other again. Not only will there be peace among humans but peace in the animal kingdom as well (Isaiah 11:6-9).

It Will Be a Time of Prosperity

Isaiah 35:1-10 talks about how the desert will bloom like a rose when the kingdom of God covers the earth. There will be no wildernesses or deserts anywhere. For someone who lives in California as I do, where the dominant color of the landscape is brown, it will be like living in Hawaii or the tropics where everything is lush green all the time.

It Will Be a Time of Purity

Starting from the top down, holiness will pervade the earth. When a king who is holy is ruling, that influence of holiness tends to extend to every other part of his kingdom. This is one of the areas where the Scriptures speak most plainly about the kingdom of God on earth (Isaiah 11:9; 25:9; 66:23; Zechariah 13:2). There will be no lack of people worshipping God and pursuing righteousness.

It Will Be a Time of Perpetual Health

Isaiah 65:20 says in that day a person a hundred years old will be regarded as a child. The life spans of the first generations of humans will become the norm again, when people lived to be nearly a thousand years old. Sickness, disease, and infirmity will be done away with, and there will be no birth defects or retardation. Children will be born abundantly, and the population will increase rapidly, filling the earth with a healthy human race.

It Will Be a Time of Personal Joy

A number of verses in Isaiah point toward the joy that will fill the earth when God is reigning over all (Isaiah 9:3-4; 12:3; 14:7-8; 25:8-9; 30:29; 42:1, 10-12). If there is anything missing in the world today (and there is much), it is true joy. I do not mean laughter; I mean the deep-seated joy that flows from a clear conscience and sense that we and the world are right with God. The pain, agony, despair, and superficial happiness that characterizes our world today will be replaced by the joy of the Lord.

Are you looking forward to a time of "peace on earth, goodwill toward men?" (Luke 2:14) It is wonderful that the peace of God can rule in our hearts today (Colossians 3:15), but it will be even more wonderful when it rules over all the earth.

APPLICATION

1. From Revelation 20:1-10, answer the following detailed questions about John's vision of a thousand year reign of Christ on earth.

   a. Who descends from heaven to earth and what does he hold in his hand? (verse 1)

   b. What does the angel do with Satan, and for how long a period? (verses 2-3)

   c. What is the purpose of the binding of Satan? (verse 3)

   d. Consider all the conflicts and tensions going on among nations today. What will happen the moment Satan is bound?

e. What is their resurrection from death called? (verse 5)

f. When do "the rest of the dead" come back to life? (verse 5)

g. What happens at the end of the thousand years? (verses 7-8)

h. What do the deceived nations do? What is the "beloved city?" (verse 9a)

i. What does God do in response? (verse 9b)

j. What happens to the devil at that point? (verse 10)

k. How long does his punishment last? (verse 10)

l. Who does the devil find already there when he arrives? (verse 10)

2. The world will be radically altered during the Millennium. What future change do you most look forward to experiencing?

a. If Christ gave you the opportunity to choose a part of life in His kingdom to rule over, what would you choose?

b. What part of this present world will you be most glad to be free of?

SPEAKING OF THE FUTURE . . .

A missionary named Henry Morrison had served some forty years in Africa and was returning to America by steamship. President Theodore Roosevelt was on the same ship and, when they entered New York harbor, there was much fanfare and celebration over the arrival of the president. Morrison felt dejected at having no one to celebrate his homecoming until a small voice came to him: *Henry, you're not home yet.*

For the Christian, the prophetic Scriptures say plainly that a permanent home is being prepared where we will dwell with God forever (John 14:2–3). While tears of discouragement or despair may blind our eyes in this life, all those tears will be wiped away when "the former things have passed away." The very things which make this life difficult—sorrow, pain, death—should serve as reminders to let the Christian know he is not home yet. For home is a place where all those things have passed away.

Don't let the tears in your eyes keep you from staying focused on your true heavenly home.

AND GOD WILL WIPE AWAY EVERY TEAR FROM THEIR EYES;
THERE SHALL BE NO MORE DEATH, NOR SORROW, NOR CRYING.
THERE SHALL BE NO MORE PAIN,
FOR THE FORMER THINGS HAVE PASSED AWAY.

—A voice from heaven in Revelation 21:4

THE GREAT WHITE THRONE JUDGMENT

Revelation 20:11-15

*In this lesson we encounter the sobering
end for those without Christ.*

You will find more in-depth information on this lesson in the
book *Escape the Coming Night,* chapter 18, pages 234-239.

OUTLINE

Somewhere in the process of explaining the Gospel to a nonbeliever,
the following objection will be raised: "I could never believe in a
God who would send someone to hell." But as clearly as the Bible
teaches that God receives believers into heaven, so it teaches He
sends nonbelievers to hell.

   I.   The Place of the Great White Throne Judgment

  II.   The Person at the Great White Throne Judgment

 III.   The People at the Great White Throne Judgment

 IV.   The Purpose of the Great White Throne Judgment
      A. The Book of Conscience
      B. The Book of Words
      C. The Book of Secret Works
      D. The Book of Public Works
      E. The Book of Life

  V.   The Punishment at the Great White Throne

OVERVIEW

Have you ever been to court to plead your case before a judge? I hope not. It is not a very enjoyable experience. The first time I went to court was a few years back after getting a traffic ticket. After a little investigation, I decided to go to court and plead my case to the judge. To make a long story short, I finally ended up paying for the ticket which is what I should have done in the first place. I discovered that the traffic court was not particularly interested in my well-reasoned arguments.

In this lesson we are going to learn about a courtroom experience far different than any on earth. As cumbersome and frustrating as it can be to go through some of our earthly court systems, many people would take a traffic court any day over the court described in Revelation 20:11-15, with one exception. The court John saw in his vision is characterized by absolute and total justice.

The Great White Throne Judgment is the final bar of justice in God's plan for the inhabitants of planet earth. Unlike earthly courtrooms, there will be a Judge but no jury, a prosecutor but no defender, and a sentence but no appeal. It is the place where sinners stand before a holy God to give an account of their sins. There is no more awesome scene presented to us in the Word of God in terms of the magnitude of its significance.

The Great White Throne Judgment is not the same as the Judgment Seat of Christ. These two judgments bring into focus two different resurrections mentioned in Revelation 20. Beginning with Christ's resurrection from the grave, the first resurrection includes the saved dead of this age who are raised at the Rapture, plus those martyred during the Tribulation, and Old Testament saints who are raised at the end of the Tribulation. All of that is the first resurrection, or "resurrection unto life." The second resurrection takes place at the end of the Millennium and includes "the rest of the dead [who] did not live again until the thousand years were finished" (20:5). This resurrection takes place a thousand years after the first resurrection and includes those dead spiritually as well as physically. This is the resurrection that leads to the Great White Throne Judgment, at which there will be no believers.

THE PLACE OF THE GREAT WHITE THRONE JUDGMENT

While we do not know where the Great White Throne Judgment takes place, we do know where it does not. It is not in heaven or on earth. It cannot take place on earth, because at the appearance of the Lord "the earth and the heaven fled away" (20:11). And it cannot take place in heaven, because no sinner can enter into the presence of God in heaven. The only answer is that this judgment takes place somewhere between heaven and earth. Perhaps the name of the throne itself is more important than its location. "Great" speaks of the Infinite One who is the Judge; "White" speaks of divine holiness, purity, and justice; and "Throne" speaks of the majesty of the One who has the right to determine the destiny of His creation.

THE PERSON AT THE GREAT WHITE THRONE JUDGMENT

The Judge upon the Great White Throne is none other than the Lord Jesus Christ Himself. He said in John 5:22 and 27 that "the Father judges no one, but has committed all judgment to the Son . . . and has given Him authority to execute judgment also, because He is the Son of Man." In Acts Peter declared that "[Christ] . . . was ordained by God to be Judge of the living and the dead" (Acts 10:42). The spiritually "living" He will judge at the Judgment Seat of Christ, the spiritually "dead" at the Great White Throne. The One upon the throne is the very One who gave His life for the redemption of those He is about to judge. He must reject those who rejected Him and His plan for their salvation.

> Consider this, you that are here present, that yet remain in an unregenerate state . . .
> When God beholds the ineffable extremity of your case . . .
> He will have no compassion upon you, He will not forbear the executions of His wrath, or in the least lighten His hand; there shall be no moderation or mercy, nor will God then at all stay His rough wind; He will have no regard to your welfare, nor be at all careful lest you should suffer too much in any other sense, than only that you shall not suffer beyond what strict justice requires.
>
> *Jonathan Edwards*

THE PEOPLE AT THE GREAT WHITE THRONE JUDGMENT

In verse 12, the phrase "great and small," describing those who stand before God and His throne, is very interesting. It is found often in the Old Testament and five times in Revelation. The phrase tells us that every class of person will be represented on that day. No position or standing in this world, or lack of it, will excuse one from judgment before God. God is not a respecter of persons. There is only one thing for which men will be judged on that day, and it is what they have done about Jesus Christ. If a person, be he great or small, has rejected Jesus Christ and has not believed on Him, he will appear before the Great White Throne. It is often alleged that the great and powerful fare better before the judges of our land than the small, but in that day all will be judged with equity.

THE PURPOSE OF THE GREAT WHITE THRONE JUDGMENT

Verse 12 tells us that when all were gathered before the Throne of God, "books were opened." There has been some confusion about the purpose of this judgment, some believing that its purpose is to decide whether a person is lost or saved. That is incorrect. Everyone appearing before the Great White Throne is lost on the basis of not placing his or her faith in Christ. This judgment is to judge the evil works of the unsaved. Men are judged from the "Book of Life" and other "books." Though we are not told specifically what the other "books" are, we have some indications from Scripture of what they might contain, that is, on what bases mankind will be judged at the Great White Throne.

The Book of Conscience

Romans 2:15 speaks of those "who show the work of the law written in their hearts, their conscience also bearing witness, and between themselves their thoughts accusing or else excusing them." This suggests that one day the human conscience may play a role in judging the nonbeliever: Did we violate our own conscience in the things we did? No person, saved or unsaved, can say that he has followed the dictates of conscience 100 percent of the time. And the conscience is not an infallible guide to what is right or wrong. But when the conscience is brazenly violated, it shows an attitude toward sin that may be brought to bear against the unbeliever.

The Book of Words

Matthew 12:36-37 says, "But I say to you that for every idle word men may speak, they will give account of it in the day of judgment. For by your words you will be justified, and by your words you will be condemned." Scientists tell us that no word we ever speak out loud is ultimately lost and that the sound waves continue on indefinitely, available to be recaptured someday. Whether that is true or not, it illustrates that once our words are spoken they can never be retrieved. They may act as the accusers of the unsaved one day at the Great White Throne Judgment. When excuses begin to be offered for past works, the Book of Words may be opened. By a man's own words he may stand condemned before the Lord.

The Book of Secret Works

The Apostle Paul taught that "God will judge the secrets of men by Jesus Christ" (Romans 2:16), and Solomon said, "For God will bring every work into judgment, including every secret thing, Whether good or evil" (Ecclesiastes 12:14). D.L. Moody, the famous evangelist, used to say that if a camera were ever invented that could take a picture of the heart of man the inventor would starve to death. No one would buy a camera that would expose the secret things of one's heart. But at the Great White Throne Judgment there will be no more secret things. Everything that men thought were secrets will be exposed before God. Those things which men thought would never be used against them because they were secrets will stand as testimonies against them.

The Book of Public Works

Paul speaks also of men "whose end will be according to their works" (2 Corinthians 11:15). Jesus said "the Son of Man will come in the glory of

> *They will die the second time. From the second death there is no resurrection. They will be sent out into the wide universe into the outer darkness.*
> *They will be wandering stars to whom the blackness of darkness is reserved forever. They will wander through this unlit darkness of eternity as derelicts of humanity, tossed upon an endless and shoreless sea; souls that have missed the purpose for which they were created—union and fellowship with God.*
>
> *Dr. I.M. Haldeman*

His Father with His angels, and then He will reward each according to his works" (Matthew 16:27). God will have a complete record of every moment of every person's life, not only their secret words but also their public works. Who a man is will be born out by what he has done, how he has lived.

The Book of Life

This is no doubt the most important of the books that will be opened. The Book of Life is mentioned a number of times in the Bible (e.g., Exodus 32:32-33; Psalm 69:28; Daniel 12:1; Philippians 4:3; Revelation 3:5; 13:8; 17:8; 21:27; 22:19). Many of those passages are in contexts dealing with believers, not unbelievers. This obviously raises the question of whether a Christian can have his name blotted out of the Book of Life. Some first century cultural background will aid our understanding of this question.

Cities in John's day had a city register which listed the names of every citizen. If a person committed crimes, or otherwise defiled his standing in the city, he could be called before a tribunal and his name removed from the city registry, literally blotted out. He would no longer be considered a citizen of that metropolis and would live from then on in anonymity or be forced to move elsewhere. I believe that concept forms the background for the Book of Life as John describes it. It is a book originally containing the name of every person ever born into this world. If that person dies having rejected God's offer of salvation, his name is blotted out of the Book of Life. It is a sobering thing to think about a person paging through God's Book of Life in vain looking for his name and not finding it.

William R. Newell, a great scholar and commentator on Revelation, said there are four things to be noted about the Book of Life:

1. It is the absence of one's name, not one's good works, that dooms a person.

2. Evil works are not the issue. Many of earth's greatest sinners' names are recorded in the Book of Life because they accepted God's offer of salvation.

3. Those whose names do not appear in the Book are cast into the lake of fire (20:15).

4. All names found in the Book were written before the judgment day. There is no record of names being recorded (decisions being made) on that day. [1]

A final purpose we can mention for the Great White Throne Judgment is to determine degrees of punishment. It is a little-known fact among Bible students that there are degrees of punishment in hell. Jesus taught by a parable in Luke 12:47-48 that those who are given more will be held more accountable than those given less. We can only conclude that some will be held more accountable by God, and therefore punished more severely, than others. For example, a person who has continually rejected, time after time, a clear presentation of the Gospel will be held more accountable by God than someone who has never heard the Gospel clearly.

THE PUNISHMENT AT THE GREAT WHITE THRONE

Both here, in verse 14, and in Matthew 25:41, 46, the concept of eternal punishment in hell is taught. It is not a popular doctrine, but it is a plain one in Scripture. Jesus spoke three words about hell for every one word He spoke about heaven. It was His compassion that prompted Him to warn men of that punishment to come if they did not accept God's salvation. Sometimes I wonder if the reason God does not allow believers to be present at the Great White Throne Judgment is because we would not be able to bear the looks of unsaved friends or relatives when they asked, "Why didn't you tell me?"

If there is someone you know whose name, as far as you know, will not be found in the Book of Life, won't you tell him soon about salvation in Jesus? Whether they choose Jesus is their responsibility, but whether they have the choice may be yours.

APPLICATION

1. In John 3:36, what is the basis for God's judgment coming upon a person?

    a. In light of the mention in the verse of "everlasting life," what can we assume is the meaning of "the wrath of God"?

    b. What is the basis for avoiding God's wrath and receiving everlasting life?

2. Read Luke 12:42-48.

   a. From this parable of Jesus, summarize the charge given by
   the master to the faithful steward. (verse 42)

   b. What will the response of the master be if the steward is
   faithful? (verses 43-44)

   c. How might the steward choose to respond to his master's
   assignment? (verse 45)

d. And what will the master's response be in such a case? (verse 46)

e. What is the point of the parable? (verse 47)

f. What is the corollary principle? (verse 48)

g. Summarize the overall point of the parable. (verse 49)

h. What is the overall context of Jesus' words in this portion of Luke's gospel? (verse 40)

i. Since the focus is on the end times when Christ returns, how would you apply this parable to the judgment He will execute at His return?

j. How would you apply this parable to nonbelievers in the world today (e.g., those in countries where the gospel has been preached widely versus countries where there has been little evangelism)?

k. What are your feelings about the principle of "relative punishment" as taught in this parable?

3. Read Romans 2:12-16.

a. Who are the two categories of people Paul is describing in verse 12?

b. What will be the standard of judgment for each group? (verse 12)

c. Which is more important in God's sight—to have (hear) the Mosaic law or to live a life consistent with the Mosaic law? (verse 13)

d. When people who haven't been taught the will of God actually do the will of God, what do their actions become to them? (verse 14)

e. What do their actions demonstrate? (verse 15)

f. Whether a man lives by the revealed will of God or the law of conscience, why will he not be granted eternal life on that basis? (James 2:10; 4:17)

SPEAKING OF THE FUTURE . . .

Here's a way to have a prophetic Christmas celebration: Try reading through Revelation 19 by the Christmas tree. It's a tradition to read about the first coming of Jesus from Luke 2 every Christmas, but it makes for an interesting contrast to read about His Second Coming from Revelation 19.

Jesus' first coming was accompanied by an angelic host announcing peace on earth. But of His second coming it is said, "In righteousness He judges and makes war" (Revelation 19:11). He came the first time as a babe in a manger, but He will come the second time as a warrior on a white horse (verse 11). The first time, He was wrapped in swaddling clothes; but when He comes again, He'll be "clothed with a robe dipped in blood" (verse 13).

At Jesus' first coming, He was surrounded by cattle, sheep, shepherds, and Magi. When He comes again, He will be surrounded by the armies of heaven (verse 14). From His mouth in Bethlehem came a baby's soft cry. But Revelation 19:15 says, "Now out of His mouth goes a sharp sword."

When Christ comes again, it will be as King of Kings, Lord of Lords, the long-awaited Sovereign, the final Judge. For His followers, it will be a day of crying, "Alleluia!" (verse 1). For those who oppose Him, it will be a day of crying "Alas!" (Revelation 18:19).

> WHEN HE COMES, IN THAT DAY,
> TO BE GLORIFIED IN HIS SAINTS . . . .
>
> —Paul in 2 Thessalonians 1:10

Note:
[1] William R. Newell, *The Book of The Revelation, 9th edition* (Chicago: Moody Press, 1953), 334.

THE NEW HEAVEN AND THE NEW EARTH

Revelation 21:1-22:5

*In this lesson we learn about the New Jerusalem,
our eternal home.*

You will find more in-depth information on this lesson in the
book *Escape the Coming Night,* chapter 19, pages 241-246.

OUTLINE

If most Christians knew heaven was a city, they might have second
thoughts about going, until they found out what kind of city it is.
The description John gives of the New Jerusalem portrays a
heavenly home so pure, so righteous, and so glorious that "city"
hardly does it justice.

   I. **The New Heaven and New Earth**

  II. **The New City**
       A. The Dimensions of the City of God
       B. The Description of the City of God

 III. **The Denial to the City**

Wecome now to the part of the Book of Revelation where
the heavy cloud of judgment is lifted and the people of
God get a glimpse of their inheritance. Revelation 21
is a chapter filled with good news for God's people. Many scholars
believe heaven is a continuation and perpetuation of the heavenly
city John describes in his vision, so studying that beautiful city will
give us our first look at our eternal home with God.

Heaven is going to be a reality for us beyond all expectation, a
place where there is no more pain, no more weeping, and no more
death. Dwelling forever in the presence of God the Father, the
Lord Jesus Christ, and the Holy Spirit is something God intended
from the beginning of His creation, but which His creation has
had to wait thousands of year to experience.

There will be a new heaven, a new earth, and a new Jerusalem.
Revelation 21 introduces us to all things "new" which the Father
has prepared for those who love Him. The old things have passed
away and all things are made new.

THE NEW HEAVEN AND NEW EARTH

Verses 1 and 5 repeat the theme that, after the Great White
Throne Judgment, God makes all things new. As wonderful as
that proposition sounds, there is surprisingly little recorded in
Scripture on what happens when God makes the new heaven and
new earth. John does tell us that the new earth he saw had no sea,
and that is definitely new! Imagine a planet with no oceans or
similarly large bodies of water.

The scientist-theologian Dr. Henry Morris offers an interesting
view on the lack of water on the planet:

"There will, in fact, be no need for a sea on the new earth. The
present sea is needed . . . as a basic reservoir for the maintenance of
the hydrologic cycle and the water-based ecology and physiology
of the animal and human inhabitants of the earth. In the new earth,
however, there will be no animals at all, and presumably all men
and women who live there will have glorified bodies with no more
need of water. Their resurrected bodies will be composed, like that
of the Lord Jesus, of flesh and bone (Luke 24:39; Philippians 3:21)
but apparently with no need of blood (1 Corinthians 15:50) to serve
as a cleanser and restorer of the body's flesh as at present. This,

in turn, eliminates the major need for water on the earth (blood is about 90 percent water, and present-day human flesh about 65 percent water)."[1]

The Apostle Peter offers another insight on the new heaven and new earth, that righteousness will dwell there (2 Peter 3:13). That will definitely be new, a world where righteousness, not unrighteousness, dwells. Isaiah 66:22 says the new heaven and earth will "remain before [God]," meaning they will be eternal. There will be no more upheavals or judgments upon the earth.

How is God going to bring the new heaven and earth into existence? Some people refer to 2 Peter 3:10-12 and suggest heaven and earth will be renovated by great heat and fire. In the nuclear age, a global conflagration is not out of the realm of possibility. But I really do not think God is planning to blow the globe up and start over. Rather, I think God is going to remake, renew, refresh, or refurbish the existing heaven and earth. Somehow, through a cleansing fire, every evil and polluted and carnal thing will be cleansed from the planet. Just like we can clean something old so that it becomes "new" again, so I believe God will cleanse the planet and make a new heaven and earth in which we will dwell for eternity.

The Bible does not tell us too much more than that about the establishment of the new heaven and earth. It will follow the Great White Throne Judgment at the end of the Millennium and will be a renovation of this present heaven and earth by fire. And with the new earth will come a new city.

THE NEW CITY

The longing for a city from God goes all the way back to the book of Genesis. We learn in the Book of Hebrews that Abraham, during the time of his sojourns, "waited for the city which has foundations, whose builder and maker is God" (Hebrews 11:10). Every saint of God can give testimony to longing for something beyond this life, but it is not until we get to Revelation 21 and 22 that we see what it is. The question is "How do we interpret what John has written down about the new city?"

We have touched on the question of interpretation, the science of hermeneutics, in previous lessons and concluded that, when the normal, literal sense of the Bible makes sense, we do not seek any other sense. We may not understand all that we take literally, but that does not mean we should not interpret it that way. Some of what you are about to discover will be hard to believe, but we will just read the Bible as it was written, starting with the dimensions of the new city.

The Dimensions of the City of God

To accommodate all the saved individuals since the beginning of time, the city will have to be large, to say the least. Verses 15 and 16 give the basic dimensions as a cube, about 1,500 miles per side, depending on how one translates the exact measurement of a "furlong." That is, think of a box whose height, width, and length are exactly the same, 1,500 miles each. That means the area on which it sits would comprise 2,250,000 square miles. But since it is a cube, the total volume of the city is 3,375,000,000 cubic miles. One writer discovered that the base of the city is roughly ten times the size of countries like France and Germany, and forty times the size of England.

> There is a sermon in the fact that the gates are pearl. Heaven is entered through suffering and travail, through redemption and blood, through the agony of a cross. A pearl is a jewel made by a little animal that is wounded. Without the wound the pearl is never formed.
>
> *David Jeremiah*
> ***Escape the Coming Night***

How would it work, living in a city that is a cube? Our minds go immediately to the concept of different levels as in a tall office building. But we do not have any idea of exactly how the city will work or be arranged. We just have to take by faith that the "mansion" Jesus has been preparing for us is going to be like nothing we have ever seen (John 14:2-3).

The Description of the City

What does all that size look like? John gives more detail on the description of the city.

1. A Holy City

The city of God is a holy city by definition. No city currently on planet earth could be the city of God because all cities are unholy. Our cities have sin and filth and pollution and crime and poverty and disease and anger and turmoil; they are not cities of God. But the new city will have none of those things; it will be a holy city. There will not be even one small white lie told in that city, no word of boasting, not the slightest sound of arguing.

Why? Because every resident will have been made holy by the redeeming grace of God and will stay that way for eternity. Because God and everyone in the city is holy, the city itself will be a holy city.

2. The Pearly Gates

"The pearly gates" has become so much a part of colloquial language that most people do not know that description is right out of Scripture: "the twelve gates were twelve pearls: each individual gate was of one pearl" (21:21). Now you can see why some commentators do not think we should read these chapters literally. Where would a pearl the size of a city gate come from? The answer is, from God, not from an oyster. If that is what God wants the gates to be of, He will make pearls the right size.

The pearl gates have the names of the twelve tribes inscribed on them and are part of the wall around the city, made of jasper. The purpose of the walls is not to keep people in or out. They simply define the dimensions of the city. Remember that all enemies have been done away with and there is no need for protection. The gates are open for access at any time.

3. The Foundations of Precious Stones

Verses 19 and 20 describe the foundation of the city wall which consists of 12 precious stones common to the time John wrote. We are not familiar with many of these stones today and so have a hard time picturing exactly what the 12 foundations look like. But from the studies I have read where researchers have tried to identify the appearance of these ancient stones, it sounds more beautiful than anything we could imagine. I think these 12 foundations are not individual, one here and one there, but are laid on top of one another. Can you imagine the blending and assimilating of 12 strata of beautiful and precious stones with the light penetrating them and reflecting off of them?

It is so appropriate that the city of God reflect the beauty of the Son of God and the infinite blessings of the redemption He

> *In heaven, how wonderful it will be to talk with the parents, children, relatives, and friends we have lost for a time during our earthly life. If someone near and dear to you has died, each day you live brings you closer to seeing him again. The years of loneliness without those we love will be erased. We will have forever to love and be loved.*
>
> *David Jeremiah*
> **Escape the Coming Night**

provided. The enormity and creativity the city of God reflects is a picture doing justice to the majesty and creativity of our God.

4. The Streets of Gold

In addition to the pearl gates, the most frequently debated part of the new city is the streets, since John says they are made of pure gold (21:18, 21). The pure gold we see in our world is not "like transparent glass," as John describes the gold in the new city, it is opaque. Somehow, it is so pure light does not reflect off it. Rather it seems to go right through it, like golden glass. We speculate in this area about things we have never seen or experienced before and can only conclude that the brilliance and beauty of this kind of gold is simply a reflection of the beauty of God Himself, indescribable.

As for the light that streams through this translucent gold of which the city and streets are made, it is not the light of the sun or the moon. Verse 23 says the city is illuminated solely by the glory of God. There is often light associated with the appearance of God in the Bible, but it is not light as we think of it, light produced by some combustible fuel always in need of replenishment. It is more like the light that came from the burning bush which Moses encountered, which did not consume the bush. It is the light of glory, not of heat or fire.

5. A Tree of Life

The last descriptive element we will note is actually in the first two verses of chapter 22: the Tree of Life. Crystal-clear water flows from the throne of God on either side of which was the Tree of Life. That which was taken away in the Garden of Eden is here restored. The Tree which was forbidden to our forefathers is now abundantly available to the residents of the city of God.

A tree bearing fruit obviously raises the question about eating in heaven. Will we be able to? When the angels visited with Abraham, they ate a meal (Genesis 18:8). When Jesus appeared after His resurrection, He ate fish (Luke 24:42-43). It appears that, even in heavenly bodies, we will be able to consume food and drink (Matthew 26:29). The fact that the fruit on the Tree of Life renews itself once a month would indicate that it is to be consumed. Fortunately, we will not be bothered by gluttony since we will be eating to the glory of God.

THE DENIAL TO THE CITY

If there is a sad conclusion to John's description of the city, it is to note that it will be denied to some. Verses 8 and 21 list the kinds of people who will not enter the city, and verse 27 summarizes by saying, "Only those who are written in the Lamb's Book of Life" will enter the city of God. And it will be too late to try to enter when the gates open for the first time. You must have a reservation long before that day.

Will you dwell in the City of God forever and revel in the beauty, purity, and glory of a place illuminated by the very presence of God? Do not put off making your reservation. Just because the gates of the city are always open does not mean just anyone can walk in.

APPLICATION

1. By the time eternity begins, God's dwelling among mankind will have been in six stages.

   a. Where was the first place God chose to dwell among His people? (Genesis 2:8-9; 3:8)

   b. Where was the second place God chose to dwell? (Exodus 25:8-9)

   c. Where was the third place? (2 Chronicles 2:1; 3:1)

d. How was the fourth place different from any preceding it? (John 1:14; the word "dwell" is the Greek word for the Hebrew "tabernacle.")

e. With the birth of the Church, how did the dwelling of God on earth change yet again? (Acts 17:24; 1 Corinthians 3:16-17; 6:19; 1 Peter 2:5)

f. What is the final place in which God will dwell with His people? (Revelation 21:1-4)

g. Identify the phrase that, throughout the ages, has expressed God's desire in relation to His people.

• Leviticus 26:12

• Jeremiah 32:38

• Ezekiel 37:27

• 1 Corinthians 6:16

• Revelation 21:3

2. Read Ecclesiastes 3:11.

   a. What has God put in the heart of every person?

   b. What does that mean?

   c. When do most people start having thoughts about "eternity?"

d. How have you identified the presence of "eternity" in your own heart?

e. What (besides death) tells you most clearly that this world is not your "true" home?

3. Read 1 Corinthians 2:9-10.

a. Which two of the five senses are mentioned by Paul? (verse 9)

b. Using our senses and our minds, how much of what God has prepared for His people are we able to imagine or conceive?

c. What surprises you most about the way John describes heaven in Revelation 21?

d. How was that revealed to us? (verse 10)

SPEAKING OF THE FUTURE . . .

L ike an eager bride, we as the church are waiting for our Bridegroom. One author has pictured the church as a young lady waiting for her love to return.

J. A. Seiss writes about a maiden whose true love left her for a voyage to the Holy Land. He promised on his return to make her his beloved bride. Many told her that she would never see him again. But she believed his word, and every evening she went down to the shore to kindle a beacon light to welcome the returning ship. By that watchfire, she prayed for the winds to hasten on the sluggish sails, that he who was everything to her might return.

Even so, Jesus has gone away to heaven, promising to return to make us His bride. Some say that He is gone forever, and that we shall never see Him again. But His last words were "Surely, I am coming quickly."

Let us remember that we are the bride waiting on the shore for our Lord to return. One day, like that maiden, our hearts will rejoice when our Bridegroom returns.

COME, I WILL SHOW YOU THE BRIDE, THE LAMB'S WIFE.
—An angel in Revelation 21:9

Note:
[1] Henry M. Morris, *The Revelation Record* (Wheaton, IL: Tyndale House Publishers, Inc., 1983), 437.

WHAT WILL WE DO IN HEAVEN?

Revelation 21:1-22:5

In this lesson we learn what will, and will not, be in heaven.

You will find more in-depth information on this lesson in the book *Escape the Coming Night*, chapter 19, pages 246-249.

OUTLINE

The best way for a person who has a Biblical worldview to imagine what heaven is like is this: The absence of everything that breaks the heart, burdens the soul, and grieves the spirit and the presence of everything that rejoices the heart, refreshes the soul, and lifts the spirit—forever.

    I.   There Will Be No Sanctuary in Heaven

    II.   There Will Be No Sun in Heaven

    III.   There Will Be No Sickness in Heaven

    IV.   There Will Be No Sadness in Heaven

    V.   There Will Be No Separation in Heaven

    VI.   There Will Be No Sin in Heaven

    VII.   There Will Be in Heaven . . .
        A. Singing
        B. Serving
        C. Sharing

I read a story once about a little blind girl whose idea of the beauty of the world was based solely on what her parents had told her. A surgical procedure was developed which would allow her to regain her vision and she regained her eyesight. After her convalescence, the day came for the bandages to be removed from her eyes. The first person she saw was her mother, and after embracing her she went immediately to the door to look outside. For the first time she saw the beauty of creation. She turned to her mother and exclaimed, "Mama, why didn't you tell me it was so beautiful?"

Of course, her mother had done her best to describe the world in the most colorful ways possible, but the fact is "a picture is worth a thousand words." And I think someday when we get to heaven we are going to have the same reaction that little girl did— "John, why didn't you tell us it was going to be so beautiful?" I do not know that anyone, in the limited space in which John the Apostle wrote, could have described heaven any better. But his description will fall far short of actually being there.

When we consider "being there," the next question is "What will we do in heaven once we are there?" One of the best ways to think about that is in terms of the words the Bible uses to describe heaven itself. When it is referred to as a "country," we think of its vastness. When it is called a "city," we think of inhabitants. Calling heaven a "kingdom" suggests the orderliness and structure of rule and authority. "Paradise" makes us think of beauty. But if there is one word that makes us think about what we will actually do there, it is the word "house" (John 14:2).

"House" makes us think of home and family and relationships and living. We live in a house here on earth, so what will life in our heavenly house be like? There are six things, among others, that will not be in heaven, and three that will.

THERE WILL BE NO SANCTUARY IN HEAVEN

There will be no sanctuary or tabernacle or temple in heaven— and no churches. Revelation 21:3 and 22 say that "the Lord God Almighty and the Lamb are its temple." Because God will be dwelling in the midst of His people, just as He started off doing in the Garden of Eden, there will be no need for a sanctuary for Him to dwell in.

We incorrectly call our churches "sanctuaries" today because they are where we draw together once a week to worship God and hear His Word proclaimed. But God does not dwell in buildings in this age; He dwells in His people. At present, we cannot "see" His presence as we will be able to in heaven. Instead of dwelling "in" us in heaven, He will dwell "among" us, in our very presence! No building or structure could improve on His very presence in our midst.

The same Jesus who healed the sick, raised the dead, fed the multitudes, died on Calvary, was raised from the dead, and who ascended into heaven will be walking among us in heaven. We will have unbroken, personal fellowship with Him forever.

THERE WILL BE NO SUN IN HEAVEN

Revelation 21:23 says plainly there will be no sun or moon in heaven to provide illumination, because "the glory of God illuminated it. The Lamb is its light." We forget sometimes that there was light before God said, "Let there be light" (Genesis 1:3). God Himself is light "and in Him is no darkness at all" (1 John 1:5). Jesus said we are the light of the world (Matthew 5:14) but in reality we are only reflectors of His light. He is the only source of eternal light, for even our sun is slowly dying out. Light in heaven for eternity would have to come from the Light which is God Himself.

No sun or moon means there will be no night. We will live constantly in the light in heaven. Think what that means for our lives: continual, uninterrupted fellowship and activity. The depression and discouragement that often accompanies the darkness will nowhere be found in heaven.

THERE WILL BE NO SICKNESS IN HEAVEN

Like every church, we have members in our congregation who struggle with significant health challenges. My heart goes out, personally and as their pastor, to them as they suffer. Having had my own bout with cancer, I am all too able to identify with the frailty our bodies manifest as we walk through this wounded world.

Whenever I am in pain, or meet with someone who is, my thoughts go immediately to the day described in 21:4, a day when there will be no more tears, death, sorrow, crying, or pain. All of us are touched by the pain of sickness and infirmity, both physical and emotional. Whether it touches us or someone we care about, all of us have reason to anticipate a pain free heaven.

Think of it. Those today who are blind, deaf, lame, mute, congenitally impaired or deformed . . . all will receive completely whole resurrection bodies for their eternal stay in heaven. All doctors, nurses, pharmacists, therapists, and undertakers will be out of business forever!

> *There are no stonecutters chiseling epitaphs in glory. There are no wreaths on the mansion doors in the sky. There are no graves on the hillsides of heaven. There are no obituary columns in the newspapers. There are no funeral processions over the streets of gold. There is no sadness in heaven.*
>
> *David Jeremiah*
> **Escape the Coming Night**

THERE WILL BE NO SADNESS IN HEAVEN

Verse 4 also says, by the wiping away of tears, there will be no sadness in heaven. That promise was made initially in 7:17 where John saw the Lamb wiping away all the tears from the eyes of the saints. But if there are no tears in heaven, what tears is he wiping away? I mentioned this in an earlier lesson, but it never hurts to call it to mind again. These are the tears resulting from the judgment seat of Christ.

Believers are not judged as to salvation at the judgment seat of Christ but as to their faithfulness to Christ. And I think there will be many tears shed at that time. Just as Peter "went out and wept bitterly" over his own failure to be loyal to Jesus (Matthew 26:75), so many of us will weep at things done which we ought not to have done, and things left undone which we ought to have done. Wasted opportunities, broken promises, words spoken in anger, sins not repented of—all will be brought to the fore and result in tears in the eyes of believers. Thankfully, those tears will be temporary as our forgiving Savior wipes them away.

THERE WILL BE NO SEPARATION IN HEAVEN

Have you ever realized that, in heaven, you will never again be separated from the ones you love? Just as space and time did not seem to be an issue with Jesus in His resurrection body, neither do I think it will be an issue for us. Geography will be a moot point in heaven; we will be able to be in the presence of anyone at any time.

This was probably a poignant moment for the Apostle John as he came to this realization recording the vision of heaven. He was exiled on the island of Patmos in the Aegean Sea, having been sent there to die by the Roman Emperor Domitian. Those in the household of faith in Ephesus were separated from him by an expanse of water which was unbridgeable. John was totally cut off from those he loved and longed to serve as an apostle. He no doubt lived every moment in lonely anticipation of being reunited with loved ones, if not on earth, then certainly in heaven.

Anyone who travels sees the pain of separation constantly in airports as family and friends say goodbye to one another one more time. For believers, that pain will soon disappear forever.

THERE WILL BE NO SIN IN HEAVEN

John names categories of sinners in verses 8 and 27 who will not find their way through the pearl gates into the heavenly city. Revelation 22:15 says they are "outside" the city, or shut out of it. Why? Because there is no sin in heaven, and therefore no sinners. Only those who have chosen to be forgiven their sins will enter heaven. It is not that they never sinned. All have sinned. Rather, they accepted God's offer of forgiveness for their sins.

Theologically, the reason there is no sin in heaven is because of what 22:3 says: "And there shall be no more curse." When Adam sinned, all creation fell under a curse resulting from sin (Genesis 3:17-19). But because Christ redeemed us from the curse of the law when He died on Calvary, we enter heaven free from propensity (ability) to sin, the proclivity (tendency) to sin, and the penalty (continual sinning and ultimate death) of sin.

We do not even know what it would be like to pick up our daily newspaper and not find one instance or example of sin being reported for we know if it is out there, the media will report it! We are starting to see things happen in our high schools now that used to happen in the world of gangsters and hoodlums. We hear occasionally about the decrease in certain kinds of crime, yet somehow we have no overall sense that sin is decreasing in our society. Instead, it seems all the more prevalent and pervasive. But a day is coming when it will be gone forever.

THERE WILL BE IN HEAVEN . . .

It is good to revel in the absence of negative things in heaven. No one could deny his or her excitement about being free for eternity from much of what burdens us in this life. But if we take off our "worldly garments," what shall we put on in their place?

Singing

The Book of Revelation has more songs than any other book of the Bible except Psalms. That gives us a clue as to what the priorities in heaven are, doesn't it? Anyone who has ever had the privilege of singing in a large choir of hundreds and hundreds of people, perhaps in a very large church or at an evangelistic crusade, knows the power and thrill that comes from voices united in worship and praise. The first day I attended chapel in seminary and heard 700 men singing together in unison was one of the most moving

> *Our service will be according to our tastes and our ability. We will do tasks happily, without weariness.*
> *Many people hate what they're doing on earth—they don't like their jobs, their bosses, the places in which they work. But our service in heaven will be just the opposite. We'll love every eternal minute of it.*
>
> *David Jeremiah*
> ***Escape the Coming Night***

experiences I have ever had. Those experiences are only a foretaste of the perfectly pitched praises we will offer to the Lord forever.

Serving

There is an important, probably often overlooked, phrase in 22:3: "and His servants shall serve Him." It comes in the context of the throne of God and the Lamb of God and suggests a priest-like service of worship in the presence of God. Service is not a new concept in Revelation. All who have been used by God on earth or in heaven have been referred to as servants (1:1; 7:3; 10:7; 11:18; 15:3; 19:5; 22:6). To be called, or known as, a servant is one of the most honoring titles in Scripture. What will we do to serve God in heaven? I think we are going to get to do exactly what would fulfill the desires of our heart, that thing which we feel most fulfilled doing, that thing we always thought we were "made to do."

Sharing

Heaven is going to be the greatest experience of fellowship you have ever had. All of your friends in Christ, plus millions more you have never met, will be there. The Father, Son, and Spirit will be continually available. The saints from the pages of the Old Testament and the New Testament will be on every corner of the Holy City. Perhaps you have a couple of favorite personages from the Bible or the pages of church history with whom you would like to chat. You will have unlimited time to do so when we get to heaven. If all of us would become as excited about those future meetings as we are the lunch or shopping date we have with a good friend this week, our whole perspective on heaven would change. Think about who you are going to get to fellowship with!

You are going to love heaven. I look forward to meeting you there and learning about everything God has done for you.

APPLICATION

1. Read 1 Corinthians (6:9-11.

   a. List the people Paul says will not inherit the kingdom of God.

   b. To whom is Paul addressing these words? (Believers or unbelievers?)

   c. What does he say some of them "were"? (verse 11a)

   d. What made it possible for them to enter the kingdom of God? (verse 11b)

e. So what makes the difference between those "fornicators" who will enter the kingdom and those who will not?

f. What warning concerning deception does Paul issue to the believers? (verse 9)

2. Read Deuteronomy 27:14-26.

a. Summarize the kinds of things which would incur a "curse" in the Old Testament.

b. Is there anyone who has not been cursed? (Psalm 14:1-3)

3. Read Galatians 3:10-14.

   a. What is the basic failure of man which incurs God's curse? (verse 10)

   b. Can anyone be justified before God who has been cursed? (verse 11)

   c. What has Christ done for us? (verse 13a)

d. How did he do it? (verse 13b)

4. Read Hebrews 12:22-24.

   a. How is heaven described? (verse 22a)

   b. List all the different residents of heaven which are mentioned. (verses 22b-24)

Who is the center of attention at a wedding in our culture? Without a doubt, it's the bride. All eyes are on her as she gracefully walks down the aisle dressed in a beautiful gown. Her eyes light up as she looks into the face of her groom.

The Bible uses this picture of the bride and groom to illustrate the close relationship between the church and Christ. To better understand the significance of this comparison, we need a bit of background on a Jewish wedding. In a Jewish marriage (with apologies to today's women), the groom was the most important person in the ceremony. His presence far outweighed the bride's.

This imagery shows us who will be the center of attention when Christ comes back for His bride. The Bridegroom, Jesus Christ, will stand above all others. The bride (the church) must take second place to the blessed Lamb of God. You don't have to wait until that great event to honor the Bridegroom. As you wait for Christ's return, make Him the center of your attention today.

Gender is not an issue in the bride of Christ. Every believer will be joined to Christ the Bridegroom.

CHRIST ALSO LOVED THE CHURCH . . .
THAT HE MIGHT PRESENT HER TO HIMSELF A GLORIOUS CHURCH,
NOT HAVING SPOT OR WRINKLE OR ANY SUCH THING.

—Paul in Ephesians 5:25–27

WHAT TO DO UNTIL THEN

Revelation 22:6-16

In this lesson we learn what to do while we wait for the return of Christ.

You will find more in-depth information on this lesson in the book *Escape the Coming Night*, chapter 20, pages 251-254.

OUTLINE

It is easy to become so focused on our daily calendar that we lose sight of the calendar of the ages. From God's perspective, there are two events which govern everything else: the first and second comings of Christ. The first has happened, so we should live in light of the second.

I. **We Are to Walk Submissively**

II. **We Are to Worship Triumphantly**

III. **We Are to Witness Urgently**

IV. **We Are to Work Fervently**

V. **We Are to Watch Expectantly**

OVERVIEW

As we begin our study of the final chapter of Revelation, we can step back and look at the grand scope of the book and say the global purposes of God have been completely fulfilled. The rebellion of angels and the men they inspired is over and they have been consigned to the Lake of Fire. Jesus Christ, the King of Kings and Lord of Lords, is on His throne and His eternal reign has begun. In the universe, sin has been replaced by righteousness. The redeemed are in glory with the Lamb slain before the foundation of the world. Every good and perfect promise of God has been realized.

The final words of John's prophecy are a sort of appendix, an epilogue, to all that has come before. Chapter 1 and chapter 22 of Revelation serve as prologue and epilogue, bookends that introduce and bring to a conclusion all that is contained between, and they are remarkably similar in many ways. There are six parallel threads which run through both the opening and closing chapter of Revelation.

1. In both chapters we are told prophecy is from God (1:1; 22:6).
2. In both chapters the message is validated by an angel (1:1; 22:6).
3. In both chapters John is mentioned as the human agent in writing (1:1; 22:8).
4. In both chapters there is a blessing upon those who give attention to the prophecy (1:3; 22:8).
5. In both chapters imminency is the prevailing tone (1:1; 22:6).
6. In both chapters we are given titles for Jesus Christ we are to remember (1:5, 8; 22:13, 16).

What John said in chapter 1 he reiterates in chapter 22; he wants us to leave our reading of his book with principles and priorities which should inform our thinking and direct our walk. If we study the Book of Revelation for intellectual or academic purposes only, just so we'll know more about prophecy than our neighbor, we will have missed John's point entirely. In this lesson, therefore, we want to ask and answer the question, "How are we to live until the Rapture of the church takes place?" We now know what is going to take place in the future. How should we live as Christians until those things begin to unfold?

WE ARE TO WALK SUBMISSIVELY

Verses 6-7 tell us clearly that the things John has been shown and which he has recorded in his book are to be "kept." "Blessed is he who keeps the words of the prophecy of this book." At the beginning of these studies I mentioned the facts that very few Christians have ever been through a study of the Book of Revelation and that many Christians feel it is a book of the Bible just for those who like prophecy. But God places a high value on His prophetic words and expects every believer to know it and to keep it. In fact, Revelation issues a dire warning to any who would misuse the words of this prophecy (verses 18-19). These warnings are echoes of a similar emphasis on carefully attending to God's Word found in other parts of Scripture (Deuteronomy 4:2; Proverbs 30:5-6; Galatians 1:8-9).

> "And there shall be no more curse"—that's perfect restoration. "The throne of God and of the Lamb shall be in it"—that's perfect administration. "His servants shall serve Him"—that's perfect subordination. "And they shall see His face"—that's perfect transformation. "And there shall be no night there; and they shall need no candle, neither light of the sun; for the Lord giveth them light"—that's perfect illumination. "And they shall reign forever and ever"—that's perfect exultation. (Revelation 22:3-5)
>
> A.T. Pierson

When John says the person is blessed who "keeps" the words of the prophecy of Revelation, what does he mean? It does not mean to buy a Bible an "keep" it on your shelf or in a drawer or some other place of "safe keeping"! John was talking plainly about obedience to the Word of God. More than any other author, John used the word "keep" (Greek *tereo*) as a picture of obedience. Literally, the word means "to adhere to," "to follow," "to be submissive to," or "to walk under the authority of." John is saying, "Blessed is he who walk submissively under the authority of God's Word until Jesus returns." This would be consistent with other places where John used *tereo*, John 14:15; 15:10; 1 John 2:3; 5:2-3.

The top priority for all believers as we await the return of Christ is to walk submissively, obediently, to the Word of God. We are to discover God's will and then obey it. That will make you seem out of step with the prevailing culture, but that is okay.

That is one way you know you are walking in step with God. There is a price to be paid in the modern era for walking obediently to the Word of God, but it is a temporary price, and far less than the eternal price we pay if we do not.

One of the greatest commentaries in Scripture on walking obediently in the Word is Joshua, chapter 1. In two verses, God gives Joshua the formula for spiritual prosperity and success, a formula he needed as he took over leadership of the nation of Israel from Moses. Here are the principles given to Joshua about walking obediently in the Word (Joshua 1:7-8).

1. Read the Word obediently. We are to "observe" the Word of God in order "to do according to all." The purpose of reading and studying is so we may do what is pleasing to God.

2. Follow the Word exclusively. Joshua was not to mix the Word of God with pagan philosophies. He was to follow God's Words exclusively.

3. Believe the Word totally. Joshua was to do "all" of God's Word, not excise the parts he did not like or did not agree with.

4. Study the Word continually. Joshua was told to meditate on the Word "day and night." If we want continued spiritual success, we must continually submit to God's Word.

WE ARE TO WORSHIP TRIUMPHANTLY

The second priority for the believer before Jesus returns is illustrated in verses 8 and 9. Worship triumphantly. When John heard that Jesus was "coming quickly," he "fell down to worship." John could not contain himself at the thought of Jesus' soon appearing, and our response should be the same. John's consistent response to news about prophetic events is to worship (19:10). Even though in both instances John got confused about who to worship, his heart was in the right place. The angel who brought the messages to him gave him a clear imperative both times. "Worship God!" The worship of our great God is one of the consistent themes running through the Book of Revelation.

Sometimes we feel inadequate when it comes to praise and worship. We know how to sing in church, but when it comes to praising Him in our private devotions some people are at a loss. There is no better guide than the worship taking place in heaven. Heavenly worship focuses on the attributes and the actions of God, who He is and what He has done (4:8, 11; 5:9-10; 12-13; 7:10, 12; 11:15). The worship in heaven never loses sight of the fact that, throughout the prophetic calendar of the Church and the world, God is in control. He is on the throne, reigning supreme over the affairs of men, and His purposes will be carried out and brought to perfect completion. We can praise Him the same way as we wait for the return of Christ and the consummation of God's plan.

WE ARE TO WITNESS URGENTLY

John is told by an angel not to seal up the prophecy he has seen and recorded, "for the time is at hand." The revelation he has received needs to be shared with others. This is the opposite of what the prophet Daniel was told after he received his prophetic revelations: "Shut up the words, and seal the book until the time of the end" (Daniel 12:4). John's prophecy, because it builds so heavily on Daniel's, is the revealing of Daniel's prophecy as well as John's. Reading Revelation is almost like reading a commentary on Daniel, so the command given to John applies not only to Revelation but to Daniel.

Prophecy is one of the greatest evangelistic tools we have. I am amazed at pastors who have told me they never preach on prophecy; they consider it a waste of time. In truth, prophecy is one of the most effective tools we have for persuading men and women to come to Christ. The Apostle Paul said in 2 Corinthians 5:11, "Knowing therefore the terror of the Lord, we persuade men."

Anyone who can read about the coming days of Tribulation on earth and not be motivated to tell others how to escape the coming wrath of God has not been touched by the words of this prophecy.

Verse 11 means that the Word of God is the only agent for changing people's lives. People will stay in whatever condition they are in unless God's Word causes them to be changed. That is why the words of John's prophecy must not be sealed up. When men read what is coming upon the earth many

> *Robert Murray McCheyne was a great man of God who lived only thirty years. However, he accomplished more for the Lord in his short life than most of us do. He wore a watch which had inscribed on it: "The night cometh." Jesus said, "Night is coming, when no one can work" (John 19:4).*
>
> *David Jeremiah*
> ***Escape the Coming Night***

will be motivated to run to Christ to be saved. For in their present condition, they will not be allowed into God's eternal heaven.

WE ARE TO WORK FERVENTLY

Verse 12 gives us our next assignment until Jesus returns. Work fervently. If you are a Christian who has been rightly taught the Word of God, the first thing you out to think about when you consider the Second Coming is the judgment seat of Christ. Following the Rapture of the Church, appearing before that bar of judgment is the first thing believers will experience.

In my opinion, we have de-clawed the judgment of believers. In these lessons, I have been careful to point out that believers are not judged as to their salvation but as to their rewards for faithfulness. That is, they are judged for their works. But by making sure believers know they cannot lose their salvation, we have failed to emphasize appropriately the fact that we can lose our rewards. It is, after all, a judgment at which a verdict will be handed down.

The judgment seat of Christ is a very frightening thing for me to think about. To stand before the Lion of Judah and have His gaze penetrate the innermost parts of my heart and mind is not something I will anticipate if I have not been living my life for Him. The works I have done as a believer will be evaluated as to kind, motive, results. My whole Christian life is going to be judged. If I am going to receive the rewards God wants to give His faithful saints then I must work and serve Him fervently until the time of His return. Every day that I live determines how I will fare at the judgment seat of Christ. I do not want to be without crowns to cast as His feet, to be found empty-handed when it comes to rewards. I must work fervently "while it is day; the night cometh, when no man can work" (John 9:4).

WE ARE TO WATCH EXPECTANTLY

Finally, our last responsibility is to "watch expectantly." Why? Because four times in this chapter alone the soon coming of the Lord is emphasized [verses 7, 12, 17 (twice)]. The word "quickly" is from *tachus*, which means "quickly, swift, or soon," and from which we get our word "tachometer," the gauge that measures the revolutions per minute of an engine. It does not suggest "soon" in terms of the calendar but "quickly" in terms of the actual event. When the Lord does come, it will be so quickly that no one will have the opportunity to change their status or condition in light of His appearing. In other words, it will be too late to make a decision for Christ if it has not been done before He comes. He who is unjust or unrighteous will remain so (22:11). Now is the time to prepare for His coming; now is the time to open your eyes and begin watching expectantly, before it is too late.

In Joseph Seiss's commentary on Revelation, he paints a beautiful picture of a maiden whose lover has gone on a voyage across the sea. She builds a signal fire each night on the shore in anticipation of his ship's return until at last he comes to her. We are like that maiden, ever committed to the return of our Beloved, living as signal lights in a dark world until He comes, walking, worshiping, witnessing, working, and watching, all in light of His sudden return.

APPLICATION

1. Read Deuteronomy 4:1-8.

    a. What is the command Moses gives to the Israelites as they prepare to go into the Promised Land? (verse 1a)

    b. What was the purpose of the command; that is, what will be the result of their obedience to the command? (verse 1b)

    c. Conversely, what might they expect to happen if they do not obey the command?

    d. How complete was the body of revelation given by God to Moses for Israel? (verse 2)

    e. What were they not to do? (verse 2)

f. Compare this command to the warning given in Revelation 22:18-19.

g. What would be the result if a watching world obeyed God's Word? (verse 6)

h. How are the words of God to be compared with the words of any other "god?" (verses 7-8)

i. How are those words going to be manifest to the world if not through those who possess them?

j. Describe a time in your life when your adherence to the Word of God either caused you to pay some price or resulted in someone being attracted to the faith.

2. From the following verses written by inspiration from God, what insight do you get concerning the important of walking obediently according to the Word of God?

a. John 14:15

b. John 15:10

c. 1 John 2:3

d. 1 John 5:2-3

3. What is the common metaphor in each of the following verses that describes the coming of the Lord?

Matthew 24:43; Luke 12:39; 1 Thessalonians 5:2; 2 Peter 3:10

a. What is the implication of this metaphor as stated by Jesus? (Matthew 24:44; Luke 12:40)

b. How would you compare the care with which you protect yourself from thieves to the care with which you watch for Christ's return?

Do you know who Jesus Christ is?

According to Revelation 22:20, you've come to the right book—a book whose sole purpose is to unveil Jesus Christ's full identity: "Surely I am coming quickly." Once scorned as a blasphemer who simply claimed to be God, Jesus Christ is revealed in the book of Revelation as the King and Ruler of all. Once humiliated by being stripped and nailed to a cross, Jesus Christ is revealed as the Lamb that is worthy to receive all honor and blessing.

The book of Revelation is the unveiling of Jesus Christ in all His glory. Woven throughout its pages, you hear heaven proclaiming, "Yes, He is the Messiah, the Chosen One of God. Yes, He is the Savior of the world. Yes, He is the Almighty who has defeated Satan."

As you learn more about the earthly battles and heavenly victories that Jesus Christ has fought and won, may your desire to see Him clearly be accompanied with deep joy and eternal gratitude as you discover who He is and all He's done for you.

You don't have to wait for Him to be revealed in His fullness to know Him. Believe on Him now so you will be ready for His coming.

> I KNOW THAT MESSIAH IS COMING (WHO IS CALLED CHRIST).
> WHEN HE COMES, HE WILL TELL US ALL THINGS.
>
> —A Samaritan woman in John 4:25

THE LAST INVITATION IN THE BIBLE

Revelation 22:17-21

In this lesson we summarize the simplicity and availability of the Gospel.

You will find more in-depth information on this lesson in the book *Escape the Coming Night*, chapter 20, pages 254-255.

OUTLINE

We have grown so accustomed to comfortable and privileged lifestyles that we are overwhelmed by the Bible's images of judgment. The world, minus the Church, is headed for catastrophic days ahead which some will believe only when they see them. Better to believe now than then.

I.   The Reason Anyone Responds to the Gospel

II. The Restrictions on Anyone Responding to the Gospel

III. The Responsibility for Anyone Responding to the Gospel

IV. The Requirement for Anyone Responding to the Gospel

Forty-two lessons ago we began our study of the Book of Revelation. If you have trekked through all four volumes of the study guides on Revelation, may I say congratulations for your perseverance and hunger to know the Word. When these messages were originally preached in our church, God did great things through the words of His prophecy in Revelation. I trust the same has been true in your life as well, that you have already begun to reap the blessings promised to those who read and obey this Book.

It could not be more appropriate that the invitation to come to Christ in verse 17 comes where it does, at the end of the Bible and the Book of Revelation. It would be heartbreaking for someone to read this Book, to get a glimpse of the future through John's visions, and then leave Revelation without personally coming to know the One who is soon to come. Thus there is the invitation, "And let him who thirsts come. And whoever desires, let him take the water of life freely."

In our last lesson we learned that, until Christ comes, we are to walk submissively, worship triumphantly, witness urgently, work fervently, and watch expectantly. But before anyone can do any of those things, he must first come to Christ. Actually, there are two invitations in verse 17. First, the Holy Spirit and the Bride (the Church) say to Jesus (verse 16), "Come!" And then the last part of the verse is an invitation to all who thirst to come and take of the water of life freely. John is writing this last chapter not from heaven or from the perspective of the future, but from earth. That is where the Church is, and the Spirit which indwells the Church, as he writes. So the Spirit and the Bride say, "Come back to get your Church, Lord!"

Are you saying, "Even so, come, Lord Jesus!" (verse 20)? Some people have told me that their desire for the Lord to return increased as they got older. As their friends and other loved ones began to die and go to be with the Lord, the desire for the Lord to return increased. I know people who are persecuted for their faith today are probably saying daily, "Come, Lord Jesus!" But in reality, this world is not the true home for any believer. It groans and travails under the curse of sin. Everyone who knows the Lord should be saying, "Come quickly, Lord!"

John says that "him who hears" should say, "Come!" That is, anyone who hears or reads the words of prophecy he has written down should be responding by asking the Lord to return. Anyone with their spiritual priorities in place will long for Christ to return upon hearing the details of the Book of Revelation. Sometimes we get so caught up in our long-range plans we forget that the very best thing that could happen to us if we are believers is for the Lord Jesus Christ to return today. "Come and establish your kingdom, Lord. Rid the earth of sin. Let righteousness and truth and justice fill the earth."

This presentation of the Gospel is about as pure and uncomplicated as it gets. Are you thirsty? Then come and drink freely of living water. When we send missionaries from our churches around the world, they are taking this simple message to all who thirst. There are four things about the Gospel as expressed in this verse that we should note as we close our study of Revelation.

THE REASON ANYONE RESPONDS TO THE GOSPEL

John clearly tells us the reason why anyone comes to Christ through receiving the Gospel message about Him: They are thirsty! All human beings are born with a vacuum, an empty place in their lives, which can only be filled with living water. As people grow and begin to see their own inability to fill that space with what the world offers, and they see the collective empty space in the soul of the whole human race, they begin to identify their thirst. And then when they come in contact with someone who knows the Lord, that thirst becomes more pronounced and they identify

> Jesus answered and said to her, "If you knew the gift of God, and who it is who says to you, 'Give Me a drink,' you would have asked Him, and He would have given you living water. . . . Whoever drinks of this water will thirst again, but whoever drinks of the water that I shall give him will never thirst. But the water that I shall give him will become in him a fountain of water springing up into everlasting life." (John 4:10, 13)
>
> Jesus Christ

it as spiritual thirst. That is one of the reasons Jesus said we are "the salt of the earth" (Matthew 5:13).

Salt is a preservative, first of all, but it also creates thirst. My uncle used to put gigantic blocks of salt out for his cattle to lick so they would eat and drink more and be healthier. That is our purpose as salt in the world, to make the spiritual thirst of people around us so strong that they reach out for the living water which Christ offers. The reason we emphasize godliness and purity and commitment and walking in the truth is, first of all, out of obedience to Christ. But when we do that we so distinguish ourselves from the world that their thirst for living water becomes stronger when they see our lives. The reason people come to Christ is because they are thirsty and discover He is—not He has—living water.

THE RESTRICTIONS ON ANYONE RESPONDING TO THE GOSPEL

The restrictions on those who might come to the Christ are . . . non-existent! There are no restrictions. John says, "Whoever desires. . . ." Who can come to Christ? Anyone who wants his or her thirst quenched forever.

I often have people ask me, "How does 'whoever' fit with the doctrine of election?" The Bible does teach election, but it also teaches "whoever." Therefore, both are true. I do not pretend to understand how all of that works out in the mind of God, but that is not my job. My job is to make the Gospel attractive to the thirsty—whoever is thirsty—and trust God to work out the election part. There are thirsty people all over the world, wherever I go. So there is no shortage of opportunity to be salt to create thirst and then offer Living Water through the Gospel of Christ. Whether they get saved or not is not my business; I leave that part to God. All I have to do is say to a thirsty person, "Jesus Christ loves you and died for you and wants to fill your life with the meaning and purpose God created you to enjoy." The Bible places no restrictions on my ability and my responsibility to do that wherever I go.

If you think there is someone you have witnessed to who is "unsavable," you need to read the "whoever" verse again. Anyone who wants to be saved can be saved.

THE RESPONSIBILITY FOR ANYONE RESPONDING TO THE GOSPEL

We've talked about the Christian's responsibility to be salt to "whoever" is thirsty. But what about the responsibility of the person who is responding to the Gospel? His or her responsibility is best seen in the King James ("whosoever will") and the New King James ("whoever desires") versions of verse 17.

Where does a person get saved? In his intellect? Does he gather and retain a certain kind and amount of information and then he is saved? Is it a matter of education? Apparently not, since we all know highly educated and intelligent people who are not saved. We cannot educate people into the kingdom of God.

What about the emotions? Do people get saved because they feel saved? The danger with that is if they are having a good day they have assurance of their salvation, but if they are having a bad day they think they lost their salvation. That makes the Christian life a roller coaster experience that is foreign to the Gospel. We do not get saved in our emotions.

Before you object to what I am saying, let me acknowledge that the intellect and emotions are, of course, important in the Christian life. We do have to know certain things to be saved, and we will have emotional responses to our salvation experience. But the thirsty person is not responsible first and foremost to be smart or emotional. In the truest sense, we are saved in our will—"whoever will" or "whoever wants to." We are saved when we say, "Lord, I will place my faith in You to forgive my sins and I receive eternal life."

One of the best illustrations we have of this in Scripture is the prodigal son. This is the boy who rose up and demanded his share of his father's inheritance, then left home and spent it all on wasteful living. He had no money and ended up feeding the pigs on a farm in order to get something to eat. Then he began to think about how life had been at home, how the servants in his father's house lived better than

> On the last day, that great day of the feast, Jesus stood and cried out, saying, "If anyone thirsts, let him come to Me and drink. He who believes in Me, as the Scripture has said, out of his heart will flow rivers of living water."
> (John 7:37-38)
>
> Jesus Christ

he was living. The Bible does not focus on his intellect or his emotions. It simply records his words: "I will arise and go to my father . . ." (Luke 15:18). His deliverance out of his desperate situation came as a result, not of intellect or emotion, but of the choice of the will.

People put off believing in Jesus all the time because they "don't understand enough" or they "don't feel like it," when those are not the issues. Salvation is a choice of the will, choosing to believe in Jesus as Savior and to follow Him as Lord.

THE REQUIREMENT FOR ANYONE RESPONDING TO THE GOSPEL

Finally, the Gospel requires something of anyone coming in need of living water. Verse 17 says, "let him take the water of life." The only thing a thirsty person has to do is reach out and take the water.

Now some people will say that is just too easy; there must be more to it. There must be something I have to say, or there must be some level of maturity or goodness I have to attain, or there must be some kind of schooling or education I have to undergo. And the answer is nothing. All you have to do is take the water. Others will argue that the very act of taking the water is a form of good works, that there is absolutely nothing we do to be saved, and that it is all of grace. Well, reaching out and receiving a gift does not then mean that I did something to earn the gift. The grace part of the gift is that it is offered freely. The response of the thirsty person is simply to take that which is offered freely, by grace.

If there was anything you could do to help yourself get saved even a little bit, do you think God in heaven would have sent Jesus Christ to this earth to die on the cross for your sin? If there was any human way you could merit salvation or recommend yourself to God, do you think He would have paid the high price He did of killing His own Son as a sacrifice? He sent Jesus Christ into this world because there is not a single thing any of us can do, except take the living water that is freely offered to us. That is the one requirement. We call it by various terms—belief, trust, commitment—but it means the same as "taking" the living water and drinking deeply.

Isaiah the prophet said, "Ho! Everyone who thirsts, Come to the waters; And you who have no money, Come, buy and eat. Yes, come, buy wine and milk without money and without price.

Why do you spend money for what is not bread, and your wages for what does not satisfy? Listen carefully to Me, and eat what is good, And let your soul delight itself in abundance" (55:1-2).

As we conclude our study of Revelation, only one question remains. Have you taken the living water which God offers in the person of Christ? If so, then the Book of Revelation is for you a glorious confirmation of the fact that you will never thirst again. If you have not taken a drink of that water, may I encourage you to do so today. The Bible says, "Whoever calls on the name of the LORD shall be saved" (Romans 10:13). Call upon Him and quench your thirst, both now and forever.

APPLICATION

1. Read John 4:4-42.

   a. Who did Jesus meet at a well in Samaria? (verse 7)

   b. What was it in this woman's life that told Jesus of her thirst? (verse 18)

   c. What kind of thirst would you imagine she had, given her background?

   d. How did He use the well and water as a way to introduce her to eternal life?

e. How can you tell that the idea of "living water" did not register with her at first? (verse 11)

f. What did Jesus mean when He said that the person who drinks living water will "never thirst" again? (verse 14)

g. What kinds of "thirsts" has the living water of Christ quenched in your life?

h. What is the central "thirst" that living water quenches in the life of every person who receives it?

2. What word in 2 Corinthians 5:11 and Galatians 1:10 characterized Paul's style of evangelism?

   a. What does Agrippa's statement to Paul indicate about Paul's use of persuasion in presenting the Gospel? (Acts 26:28)

   b. How did Paul use "jealousy" to win people to Christ? (Romans 11:14)

   c. What part of humanity does God want to be saved? (2 Peter 3:9)

3. Read 1 Corinthians 9:19-23.

a. How many people did Paul attempt to win to Christ? (verse 19)

b. What was he willing to do to accomplish that? (verse 19)

c. What did he do to win Jews? (verse 20)

d. What did he do to win Gentiles? (verse 21)

e. How did he summarize his approach to "all men"? (verse 22)

f. Was there anything within the bounds of the "law toward Christ" that he would not do to win people to Christ? (verse 22)

4. What aspect of your life is the "saltiest"? What do you manifest in your life that would cause nonbelievers to desire "living water"?

Whenever there is an earthquake on America's West Coast people wonder, "Will I be ready when the next one comes?" "Am I prepared, knowing it can come at any time?"

"What changes should I make in my dwelling place, my habits, or my precautions?"

As people who love the Lord, we must likewise ask ourselves if we are truly prepared to meet Jesus face-to-face at any moment. We know that He will come again; that is for certain. What we don't know is when He will come again.

The good news is that we don't need to prepare physically for meeting Jesus. As we get ready for that glorious encounter, there's no need to purchase new clothes, get a haircut, or polish our shoes. The only thing we truly need to do is to prepare our hearts.

Is your heart—and every corner of your spiritual life—cleaned up and ready to meet Jesus like a bride perfectly adorned for her wedding day? Since you don't know when He will come, today is the best time to be sure you are ready.

Jesus said He would come like a thief—unexpectedly. The urgency in His words should compel each of us to be sure we are ready in our hearts today. Don't let anything hold you back from being fully prepared to meet the Lord.

> THEREFORE YOU ALSO BE READY,
> FOR THE SON OF MAN IS COMING AT AN HOUR
> YOU DO NOT EXPECT.

—Jesus to His disciples in Matthew 24:44

Turning Point
Resources
by Dr. David Jeremiah

Escape the Coming Night

How easy it is to dismiss the modern-day prophets who predict the end of the world. But then consider recent examples of world turmoil or the latest evidence of modern decadence, and silently wonder: Is this it? Is this a sign? Is this the end? Dr. Jeremiah offers a fresh, biblically sound explanation of the signs, symbols, prophecies, and warnings of the end times. *Escape the Coming Night* is a penetrating look at the prophetic time machine that is in the book of Revelation and a vivid reminder of how, in the face of coming darkness, we should live today.

Soft Cover Book REVBK *(Can - $20/UK - £8.50)*   **$13**

Study Guides
- Volume 1 REVSG1 *(Can - $14/UK - £6)*   **$9**
- Volume 2 REVSG2 *(Can - $14/UK - £6)*   **$9**
- Volume 3 REVSG3 *(Can - $14/UK - £6)*   **$9**
- Volume 4 REVSG4 *(Can - $14/UK - £6)*   **$9**
- 4 Study Guide Package REVSGP *(Can - $44/UK - £18)*   **$28***

Cassette Albums
- Volume 1 REVAL1 (12 tapes) *(Can - $95/UK - £39)*   **$60**
- Volume 2 REVAL2 (12 tapes) *(Can - $95/UK - £39)*   **$60**
- Volume 3 REVAL3 (10 tapes) *(Can - $79/UK - £33)*   **$50**
- Volume 4 REVAL4 (9 tapes) *(Can - $71/UK - £30)*   **$45**
- 4 Album Cassette Package REVALP *(Can - $270/UK - £112)*   **$172***

Compact Disc Albums
- Volume 1 REVAL1CD (12 CDs) *(Can - $132/UK - £55)*   **$84**
- Volume 2 REVAL2CD (12 CDs) *(Can - $132/UK - £55)*   **$84**
- Volume 3 REVAL3CD (10 CDs) *(Can - $110/UK - £46)*   **$70**
- Volume 4 REVAL4CD (9 CDs) *(Can - $99/UK - £41)*   **$63**
- 4 Album CD Package REVALPCD *(Can - $375/UK - £157)*   **$240***

ORDER 1-800-947-1993

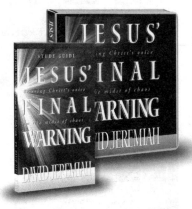

Turning Point Resources

STUDY GUIDES

All Study Guides are regularly priced at $9
An audiocassette or CD album is also available for each of the following series.
(Sold separately. Individually priced.)

Acts: The Church in Action (Volume 1)
Authentic Christian Life, The
  (1 Corinthians, 3 Volumes)
Blessings and Behavior of the Believer, The
  (Ephesians, 2 Volumes)
Celebrate His Love (Christmas)
Christians Have Stress Too
Christ's Death and Resurrection
Escape the Coming Night
  (Revelation, 4 Volumes)
Facing the Giants in Your Life
Family Factor
For Such a Time as This (Esther)
Fruit of the Spirit, The (Galatians)
Gifts from God (Parenting)
Giving to God
God, I Need Some Answers (Psalms)
God in You (The Holy Spirit)
God Meant It for Good (Joseph, 2 Volumes)
Grace of Giving, The (Stewardship)
Greatest Stories Ever Told, The (Parables)
Handwriting on the Wall (Daniel, 3 Volumes)
Heroes of the Faith (Hebrews)
Home Improvement
How to Be Happy According to Jesus
  (The Beatitudes)
How to Live According to Jesus
  (The Sermon on the Mount, 2 Volumes)
Invasion of Other Gods (New Age)
Investing for Eternity
Issues of the Home and Family
Jesus' Final Warning (Prophecy)

Knowing the God You Worship
Learning to Live by Faith (Abraham,
  2 Volumes)
Living by Faith (Romans, 6 Volumes)
Living in the Light (1 John)
Looking for the Savior (Thessalonians,
  2 Volumes)
Miracles of Christ, The
My Heart's Desire (Worship)
Nation in Crisis, A (Joshua, 2 Volumes)
New Spirituality, The (New Age)
Overcoming Loneliness
People God Uses, The
People Who Met Jesus
Power of Encouragement, The
Power of Love, The
Powerful Principles from Proverbs
Prayer—The Great Adventure
Runaway Prophet—Jonah, The
Ruth, Romance, and Redemption
Searching for Heaven on Earth (Ecclesiastes)
Seeking Wisdom—Finding Gold
Signs of the Second Coming
Spiritual Warfare
Stewardship Is Lordship
Tender Warrior, The (David, 2 Volumes)
Turning Toward Integrity (James)
Turning Toward Joy (Philippians)
What the Bible Says About Angels
When Wisdom Turns to Foolishness (Solomon)
When Your World Falls Apart (Psalms)

BOOKS

Escape the Coming Night (Revelation) $13
Gifts from God (Parenting) $19
God in You (The Holy Spirit) $19
Handwriting on the Wall, The (Daniel) $12
Life Wide Open (Purposeful Living) $19
My Heart's Desire (Worship) $19
Power of Encouragement, The $13
Prayer—The Great Adventure $13
Prayer Matrix, The $10
Sanctuary (Daily Devotional) $14

Searching for Heaven on Earth (Ecclesiastes) $22
Secret of the Light, The $15
Slaying the Giants in Your Life $13
Stories of Hope from a Bend in the Road $13
Things That Matter, The $10
Turning Toward Integrity (James) $10
Turning Toward Joy (Philippians) $10
Until I Come (Prophecy) $13
What the Bible Says About Angels $13
When Your World Falls Apart (Psalms) $13

BOOKLETS

Creative Family Living: 20 Ideas for Christian
  Family Interaction $6.50
Family Turning Points $6.50
Financial Turning Points $6.50
How to Encourage Your Children $2.50
Living Right! 25 Behaviors of a Christian $6.50
Patriotic Turning Points $6.50
Plan for Whosoever, A $2.50

Prayer for Whosoever, A $2.50
Prophetic Turning Points $6.50
Signs at the Bend in the Road $2.50
Tour of Duty $4.00
Walking Down the Romans Road $2.50
Who I Am in Christ $2.50
Your Greatest Turning Point $2.50

POSTAGE AND HANDLING CHART

For orders	Add
Up to $5.99	$1.50
$6.00-$19.99	$2.50
$20.00-$50.99	$3.50
$51.00-$99.99	$6.00
$100.00 & over	$9.00

If you would like a complete catalog
of resources available from
Turning Point, please call
1-800-947-1993 or write
Turning Point ~ P.O. Box 3838 ~
San Diego, CA 92163-1838.
You can also visit Turning Point at
www.turningpointonline.org